The Emigrant Scots

By the same author

The Making of the Highlands (Constable)

Other books of Scottish interest
Over the Lowlands (Geoffrey Bles)
Ho for the Borders (Geoffrey Bles)
Around the Highlands (Geoffrey Bles)
A Guide to Scotch Whisky (Johnston & Bacon)
Scottish Crafts & Craftsmen (Johnston & Bacon)
The Original Scotch: A History of Scotch Whisky (Hutchinson)
Scottish & Border Battles & Ballads (Seeley Service & Cooper)
The Scottish Highlanders & Their Regiments (Seeley Service & Cooper)
A Hunt Around the Highlands: On Thornton's Tour of 1784 (Standfast Press)

Historical
The Portrait of a Hunt (Hutchinson)
The Hunting Instinct (Oliver & Boyd)
The Georgian Gentleman (Saxon House)
The Victorian Gentleman (Saxon House)
The Life & Sport of the Inn (Gentry Books)
The Tenth Royal Hussars (Seeley Service & Cooper)
Soho for East Anglia: On de Rochefoucauld's Tour of 1784 (Geoffrey Bles)
Hunting & Shooting: A History of Field Sports (Weidenfeld & Nicolson)

Biography
The Country Divine: Twelve Self-Portraits (St Andrew Press)
The Perfect Victorian Hero: Sir Samuel White Baker (Mainstream)

Directories and Lexicography
A Dictionary of Sporting Terms (A & C Black)
An International Encyclopedia of Shooting (Editor: Peerage Books)
A World Directory of Scottish Associations (Editor: Johnston & Bacon)

Guides and Manuals
Groundgame (Tideline)
The Roughshooter's Sport (Tideline)
The Roughshooter's Dog (Gentry Books)
The Game Shot's Vade Mecum (A & C Black)
Gundogs: Their Care and Training (A & C Black)
An Introduction to Trout Fishing (Spurbooks)
The Complete Guide to Horsemanship (A & C Black)

A sentimentalized Victorian view of Scottish emigration at the time: 'Lochaber no more', an engraving by Charles Coulson of a painting by J. Watson Nicol.

MICHAEL BRANDER

The Emigrant Scots

Constable · London

First published in Great Britain
by Constable and Company Ltd
10 Orange Street London WC2H 7EG
Copyright © by Michael Brander 1982
ISBN 0 09 464110 2
Set in Linotron Ehrhardt 11pt by
Rowland Phototypesetting Ltd
Bury St Edmunds, Suffolk
Printed in Great Britain by
St Edmundsbury Press
Bury St Edmunds, Suffolk

To
A Michael Brander
in Hong Kong

Contents

Illustrations

Acknowledgements

It has frequently been pointed out to me in the course of my research on this book that anyone trying to cover a subject so vast is attempting the impossible, but to any Scot that is merely a spur. Despite such comments from all round the world it has been a source of continual surprise to me how many people have been enormously helpful in every part of the globe. My thanks are due to a great number of people with whom I have corresponded, or who have been of assistance in other ways, both at home and overseas. For any errors or omissions I am entirely to blame, but my particular thanks for their help with basic research and encouragement must go to:

Mr & Mrs Bruce Campbell of St Thomas, Ontario, Canada. Donald C. R. Campbell, President of the Clans and Scottish Associations of Canada, Ontario, Canada. Rev. W. R. Chalmers, MA, BD, STM, of Dunbar, East Lothian, Scotland. Mr Donald Copeland of Balaklava, S. Australia. Charles W. Ferguson of Dallas, Texas, USA. Kenneth H. Grose, MA, of Broxmouth, East Lothian, Scotland. M. Ulf M. Hagman, Secretary of the Thorburn-MacFie Society, Uddevalla, Sweden. Mr Alex Hanna, of Woking, Secretary, The Clan Hannah Society. Mrs J. M. McBride, Secretary, The Clan Donald Council of Canada, Kitchener, Ontario. Mr William MacEwen, The Clan Ewen Society, St Peter's, Nova Scotia. Dr J. S. McGivern, Regis College, University of Toronto, Canada. Major J. C. Mackinnon, of Longformacus, Berwickshire, Scotland. Mr Fergus McLarty, Recording Secretary, The Saint Andrew's Society of The State of New York, USA. Mr Alexander C. McLeod, President, the Clan McLeod Society, USA. Professor Ray McLean, St Francis Xavier University, Nova Scotia. Dr Herbert P. MacNeal, President, The Councils of Scottish Clans Association, New Jersey, USA. Mr Andrew McNeill, Secretary, The Clan MacNeil,

Ontario, Canada. Dr Earle Douglas MacPhee, MM, MA, LLD, DCL, of Vancouver. Mrs Helen McPhie, Secretary, The MacFie Clan Society of Australia. Mr George Mannion, Publisher & Editor, *The Clansman*, Ontario, Canada. Dr John S. Moir, Scarborough College, University of Toronto, Canada. Dr Robert J. Morgan, Beaton Institute, College of Cape Breton. Mr C. C. Munroe, of Ontario, President, The Clan Munro Association of Canada. Dr James B. Pressly, MD, President, The Clan Lindsay Association, USA. Mrs Alice Richardson, Secretary, The Clans of Hawaii Club. Mrs Olive Schlatter, The Canadian Club of Whitney, Ontario. Mr E. G. Sinclair, DDS, LDS, Secretary, The Clan Sinclair Association of Canada, Ontario. Dr Ronald M. Sunter, The Canadian Association for Scottish Studies, The University of Guelph, Canada. Lt Col Lord Tweedsmuir of Elsfield, OBE, FRGS, FRSA, FZS. Mr Charles B. Wallace, President, the Clan Wallace Society, Dallas, USA.

My thanks are also due to many librarians, in particular to:

The Librarian and staff of the National Library of Scotland. Miss Christine Wright and the staff of the National Library of Scotland Lending Library, Inter-Library Loans Service; and to the many librarians throughout Scotland and the UK thus involved in providing books for research. The Librarian and staff of the Edinburgh Public Library, particularly in the Scottish Department. Mr Brian M. Gall, the Librarian and staff of the East Lothian County Council Library and of the Haddington Library. The Librarian of The Alexander Turnbull Library, Wellington, NZ.

M. B.

Introduction

Only a few readers are likely to find more than pointers to their own particular origin in this book. It does not set out to offer any startling new truths about the Scots at home or abroad; it is merely an attempt to show in outline how the Scots have spread themselves around the world, and to indicate the various reasons which prompted them to leave their native country.

A subject with such vast ramifications cannot possibly be dealt with minutely in a single book of a mere 70,000 words, or even in one double that length. Each of the chapters has provided material for numerous books already and even then the subject has by no means been exhausted. This is intended therefore as no more than a general summary and introduction.

As emigrants, the Scots have been amongst the most widespread of all, penetrating to almost every part of the world and setting up their own societies and clubs wherever they have gone. There is hardly a part of the world without its pipe-bands, Burns Clubs, St Andrew's Societies, or other Scottish manifestations. The knowledge that some ancestor was Scottish brings hundreds of thousands of descendants of emigrant Scots back to Scotland annually, to see the country to which they still feel they retain some connection, however tenuous.

The reasons for emigration in the first place were many and various, although usually made with a view to earning more money, or finding a better life, but they were also generally made with the hope, however faint, of one day returning to Scotland. It was this identification with their native country, indeed usually with one particular part of their native country, which distinguished the Scots so often from their fellow emigrants. While pre-eminently wanderers, the Scots also felt a tremendous loyalty to their homeland, and never more so than when abroad. This yearning for the land of their birth was generally transmitted to their children and passed on to their grandchildren and even great-grandchildren. Thus, even when their blood has been diluted many times over and their names changed almost beyond recognition, those with Scots blood retain their feeling for Scotland and things Scottish with a singular tenacity.

Like the Scots themselves, their parent stock, the emigrant Scots are an independent, hardy lot, who have generally contributed much to their countries of adoption, usually out of all proportion to their numbers, for they have a natural ability to adapt and put down roots while still retaining a love of their homeland. By learning something about the Scottish background to emigration, the reasons which made the Scots leave their country at different periods, and the success or failure they achieved in various fields, the emigrant Scots, their descendants, and for that matter, the Scots also, may learn something of an overseas heritage of which they are all part and of which they can all be proud.

PART I

Background:
The Scots at home and emigrating

[1]

Background up to 1603

If people of Scottish descent are accepted as Scots, there are undoubtedly far more Scots living outside their own country than are actually to be found in Scotland. This has been the case for centuries, and is the result of a steady flow of emigrants from Scotland over the past hundreds of years. The reasons for the Scots leaving their own country and seeking their fortunes elsewhere may have varied over the years, but the results have remained the same. Before examining these reasons in greater detail, however, it is essential to look first at the geographical and historical background.

Like Caesar's Gaul, Scotland is frequently divided into three parts for convenience – namely the Highlands, Islands, and Lowlands – but like many such facile generalizations this presents much too simplified a picture. The Islands, it is true, can readily be accepted as a separate geographical entity, although both historically and racially they have much in common with Caithness. Yet Caithness, though one of the northernmost parts of the mainland, having much in common with the Islands, is demonstrably a part of the Scottish north-east Lowlands. Similarly Campbeltown, at the foot of the Kintyre peninsula, although well south of Glasgow, should strictly be classified as a part of the Highlands, even if originally settled by Lowlanders.

The Highlands are probably best delineated geographically by the so-called Highland Line originally introduced by Act of Parliament in 1784 as a convenient demarcation for whisky-still taxation. The boundary thus defined ran:

A certain line or boundary beginning at the east point of Loch Crinan, and proceeding from thence to Loch Gilpin; from thence . . . along the west coast of Loch Fyne to Inveraray and to the head of Loch Fyne from thence . . . to Arrochar . . . to Tarbet; from Tarbet in a supposed line straight eastward on the north side of Loch Lomond, to . . . Callander . . . from thence north eastward to Crieff. . . and to Ambleree (Amulree) and Inver to Dunkeld; from thence along the foot and side of the Grampian Hills to Fettercairn . . . and from thence northward . . . to Kincardine O'Neil, Clatt, Huntly and Keith to Fochabers; and from thence westward by Elgin and Forres, to the boat on the river Findhorn, and from thence down the said river to the sea at Findhorn, and any place in or part of the county of Elgin which lies southward of the said line from Fochabers to the sea at Findhorn.

For the sake of accuracy, rather than for purely fiscal reasons, the line should have been extended to include all the low ground south of the Moray Firth, the Black Isle and the coastal belts of Easter Ross, as well as a large part of Caithness. Thus all the coastal plain of Banff and Buchan, south through Aberdeenshire, Angus and Fife, then beneath the Ochil foothills above the Forth and Clyde valleys, should be termed Lowland. Hence the Highlands may be seen as lying primarily to the west of the Lowlands above the Forth and Clyde valleys.

It is particularly noticeable that the climate in the west is significantly different from that in the east. The east coast as a whole has a comparatively dry climate with keen east coast winds, producing people full of energy and drive, engaged either in arable farming or fishing. The west coast has a very high average rainfall, with gales amounting at times almost to hurricanes, making any form of farming other than stock-breeding almost impossible. On the other hand, the truly remarkable sunrises and sunsets associated with the west are conducive to the poetic imagination and artistic appreciation found readily in the Highland Gael but less readily in the Lowlander.

The very coastlines themselves encourage these different attitudes of life. The west coast consists of deeply indented sea lochs, and islands crowding close up on each other, with only Ireland as the immediate neighbour. The east coast contains many small safe harbours in a coastline facing towards Scandinavia and Europe, encouraging both trade and fishing.

In the circumstances it is not surprising that the great bulk of the population gravitated to the more fertile arable regions of the Lowlands rather than to the comparatively barren Highlands. It is noticeable, for example, that the greatest number of early Christian settlements and of medieval monasteries or nunneries is to be found in the fertile Lowland areas.

Not unnaturally these physical factors had their effects on the earliest settlers known in Scotland, as well as on subsequent Scottish history. The majority of the Bronze and early Iron Age settlements, for instance, are to be found along the east coast in the Lowlands. The Romans certainly penetrated as far as Aberdeenshire on the one hand and even beyond Aberfeldy in the centre, but they built their northernmost defences, the Antonine Wall, along the line of the Forth and Clyde valleys on the edge of the central Lowlands.

The principal known inhabitants of Scotland in the fifth century AD were the Celtic Picts, whose origins are obscure. They lived in the central and eastern parts of the country. In the sixth century the Scots, also a Celtic race, who finally gave their name to the country, invaded from Ireland and settled, more or less peacefully, in the western region known as Argyll. In the south-west, or Galloway, there was another race of Celts, the Britons.

The first Teutonic invasion of Scotland was that of the Angles, who settled in south-eastern Scotland. They were followed by the Norsemen from Scandinavia, who raided both east and west coasts indiscriminately. Traces of their settlements remain all along the west coast and as far south as the Moray Firth on the east coast, but it was principally in the Orkney and Shetland Islands, and in Caithness, that they settled permanently. These places remained under Norwegian sovereignty for centuries after the rest of Scotland was united under one king.

With such a hotchpotch of racial elements, it is scarcely surprising that the early years of Scottish history were filled with inter-tribal warfare. The unifying link in the end proved to be the spread of Christianity. By the ninth century the Picts had established their supremacy over the invading Angles from the south and had started to drive them back. In 844 the Picts and the Scots were unified under the rule of Kenneth MacAlpin, thus forming a united Scotland north of the Forth and Clyde valleys. In 1018, under Malcolm II, the Scots defeated the Angles at Carham on the Tweed and thus conquered the land of Lothian. In the same year Malcolm also inherited the kingdom of Strathclyde, or

Cumbria, thus effectively ruling as far south as the Solway Firth. Even so there was no respite for Scotland from continual attacks by the Norwegians in the west and the far north, or from the English in the south, quite apart from internecine warfare. With the gradual anglicizing of the southern area, it was not perhaps surprising that the more aggressive Teutonic peoples gradually drove the Celts into the mountainous regions of the Highlands, preserving the central and eastern Lowlands for themselves. Only in Galloway were the Celtic Britons pushed southwards into the south-eastern corner of the region, like their fellow Celts in Cornwall.

During the twelfth and thirteenth centuries there was one further admixture to the many strains which finally made up the Scottish race, caused by the arrival of various Norman adventurers and their followers to take up high office in church and state. Such common Scottish names as Bruce, Cummings, Fraser and Stewart, to name a few of the foremost, are of Norman origin. It was under a de Brus, a Scot of Norman origin, that the Scottish nation was ultimately united in the fourteenth century.

Only, however, after the Norwegians led by King Hakon had been utterly defeated at the battle of Largs in 1263 was the Scandinavian hold on Scotland finally loosened. From then onwards, Scotland was orientated towards Europe rather than Scandinavia. Before the end of the thirteenth century Scotland had allied for the first time with France against England, the start of the famed 'Auld Alliance' which was to last for 300 years.

The cause of this alliance, of course, was the largely unprovoked aggression of the English who sought to conquer Scotland. Under the continuous attacks of Edward I, 'the Hammer of the Scots', Scotland was forged into a truly united nation in the flames of desperation and hate, first under Wallace, finally under Bruce. The bitterness aroused then was to survive for nearly four centuries until seemingly extinguished by the Union of the Parliaments in 1707, although smouldering embers survived, and are capable of being fanned into life even today.

After the death of Edward I in 1307, Robert I, the Bruce, was able to carry all before him until his ultimate victory at Bannockburn in 1314, when Edward II's superior forces were decisively defeated by the Scots. Knights and noblemen, burghers and clansmen, Borderers, Lowlanders and Highlanders, fought alongside each other, united in their total determination to defeat the English. The independence of the Scottish nation was summed up in the famous Declaration of Arbroath in 1320, which demonstrates both the profound reaction throughout the country at the way Edward I's invading armies had behaved and also the degree of unity the Scots felt in opposing the English. It runs:

> Our nation lived in peace until the mighty Prince Edward, King of England, the father of the present king, aggressively attacked our kingdom . . . No one who did not know them from experience could describe or fully appreciate all his outrages, massacres, violence, plunder and burning . . . sparing neither age, nor sex, religion or order . . . But we have been liberated from these countless evils by our valiant Prince and Sovereign Lord Robert (Bruce) . . . to him as the author of our people's deliverance we are bound . . . and are determined to be loyal to him in everything. But if he were to abandon our cause by being ready to make us or our kingdom subject to the king of England or the English we should at once do our best to expel him as our enemy . . . and should choose some other man to be our king, who would be ready to defend us. For so long as a hundred of us remain alive we are resolved never to submit to the domination of the English. It is not for glory, wealth or honour that we are fighting, but for freedom and freedom only, which no true man ever surrenders except with his life.

In 1328, the year before Bruce died, the English under Edward III finally recognized Scotland as an independent nation, but in the ensuing 200 years or more there was to be much bitter intermittent warfare between the two countries. Even in times of official peace, the Border country on both the English and Scottish sides was liable to be raided sporadically, without any warning, by Borderers of perennially lawless disposition wishing to acquire cattle or other livestock at their neighbour's expense, and not averse to a little bloodletting in the process. In time of war the country was liable to be devastated for some considerable distance on either side of the Borders, with little mercy shown.

In such circumstances it is understandable that even where the land was suitable for agriculture in the Borders, very little could be achieved, or was attempted. Amidst wild moorland and indifferent grazing, little could be expected beyond the rearing of cattle and goats. Thus the Borders on both sides were sparsely populated; the few villages consisted mostly of turf, or at best wooden, huts with sod roofs, huddled in the shelter of the peel-towers or castles built for defence against frequent raids and invasions.

The Lowlands were not much better, since agricultural methods were primitive in the extreme. Even the townspeople subsisted by farming, keeping cattle, pigs, and goats, and cultivating strips of oats in the common land outside the town. As was the case throughout the medieval world, monastic and religious orders were the most advanced in agriculture, and where they settled the land was generally both good and well tilled. In general, however, the living standards of the great majority were extremely low.

Until the late fifteenth century Gaelic may have been fairly generally understood outside the Highlands, but James IV, who was killed at Flodden in 1513, was the last Scottish king known to speak the language. Cut off from the Lowlands not only physically by the mountains in which they lived, but also by the language barrier, it is scarcely surprising that the Highlanders developed their own way of life.

They subsisted on oatmeal and by rearing cattle and goats. In spring the women and children would drive the beasts up to the high slopes for grazing, building shielings, or turf huts, as temporary shelters until driven down by approaching winter or scarcity of grass. In the winter the cattle would be bled and the blood added to oatmeal. Such primitive practices probably remained unchanged for centuries. Occasionally a change of diet may have been obtained by hunting the red deer in the hills, or by fishing the lochs and rivers with nets.

Inter-clan rivalry and feuds led now and then to bloodshed, although this is probably much exaggerated in poetry and song. The Highlanders certainly preyed on their Lowland neighbours, raiding their cattle and farmlands. An annual payment of meal, known as 'Blackmeal', was levied by some clans in return for guaranteeing protection against such raids. The clansmen, however, provided a ready source of men-at-arms to repel the invading English, and such examples of lawlessness were generally overlooked by the authorities. With the end of the danger of

English invasion, friction between the Highlanders and their Lowland neighbours gradually increased to intolerable proportions.

The way of life in the Islands (the Hebrides off the West coast and the Orkneys and Shetlands off the north-east coast) was of necessity quite different from that on the mainland. Under Norwegian rule for hundreds of years, the Hebrides returned to Scottish sovereignty in the thirteenth century, but the Orkneys and Shetlands only came back under Scottish rule in the fifteenth century. Thus their language, names, and entire way of life inevitably resembled the Norwegian more closely than the Scottish. The islanders lived mainly by fishing and grazing sheep, subsisting on both whales and seals when they were available. It was, naturally enough, as seamen first and foremost that they lived, since the sea around them dictated their day-to-day living.

By the end of the fifteenth century, with the accession of James IV, Scotland seemed to be making progress towards prosperity. The Auld Alliance by this time had resulted in considerable trading links with the continent. The ports on the Firth of Forth, especially, had developed into important merchant centres trading with France, the Low Countries, Scandinavia, and even as far afield as Russia. Small merchant barques transported Scottish salmon, cod, herring and oysters, then famed throughout Europe, from the Firth of Forth; Scots wool, skins and leather; barrels of ale; shipments of coal from the Lothians and Fife coalfields. They returned with burgundy and claret, silks, furs, and velvets for those who could afford them, as well as such commodities as sugar, spices, and timber.

At this point all seemed to be going well for Scotland. James IV had established the rule of law, ending the Lordship of the Isles which had been a source of disaffection over the years, controlling the unruly Borderers, and encouraging industry, commerce, and the arts. The Scottish sea-captain, Sir Andrew Wood of Largo, defeated five English ships in the Firth of Forth with only two of his own. Subsequently he defeated further forces sent to avenge this dishonour. Despite such skirmishes there were encouraging signs of peace with England, since James had married Margaret, daughter of Henry VII.

Unfortunately, as a military leader James was both rash and impetuous, a fatal combination. When France once more invoked the Auld Alliance, Scotland and England found themselves at war yet again. In 1513 James crossed the border into England near Berwick and shortly afterwards came the bloody encounter with the English army at Flodden. The flower of Scotland's manhood was killed, and on James's death his son, James V, was only fifteen months old.

It was unfortunate that Scotland was bedevilled, time after time, by minors succeeding to the throne at critical periods in her history when strong government was urgently needed. From 1406 onwards, no sooner had one sovereign (as with James IV) established the rule of law and a settled way of life, than the country was plunged into confusion again, with the nobility indulging in power struggles behind the scenes. In the circumstances it is scarcely surprising that Scotland's history was often tumultuous and at times verged on the chaotic.

It might be argued that, even taking into account the effects of Flodden, James IV's reign was in the end to prove beneficial to Scotland. He may have left the country weak and defenceless with scarcely any army remaining, but he also left it economically sounder than when he came to the throne. Flodden may have claimed so many victims in the Borders that a farm near Earlston which escaped bereavement was thereafter known as Sorrowless Field, but James IV had introduced the means of keeping the peace in that area at long last. Most important of all, it was through him that in 1603, exactly 100 years after his marriage, his great-grandson, James VI, peacefully inherited the crown of England in succession to his distant cousin, the virgin Queen Elizabeth I.

At the time, however, Flodden seemed an unmitigated disaster and its effects were to be felt throughout Scotland for many years. Predictably there was a period of political chaos as the nobles vied with each other for control of the young King. In the end James V proved capable of ruling effectively by himself, but by continuing the Auld Alliance he inevitably courted trouble with England. In 1542 Henry VIII invaded Scotland, burning Roxburgh and Kelso. When James attempted retaliation his forces were routed. Shortly afterwards James died leaving his newly born daughter Mary as his heir. Once again a minor inherited the throne of Scotland at a crucial moment.

There followed the famous 'rough wooing', when Henry VIII

attempted to secure the Scots throne by enforcing the marriage of the infant Mary to his son Edward. The attempt failed, but from 1544 to 1547 the Scots were subjected to periodic invasions. Edinburgh and Holyrood Palace were burned in 1544. In 1545 the abbeys of Kelso, Melrose, Dryburgh, and Eccles were destroyed and in 1547, even after Henry's death, the English again invaded Scotland, ravaging and burning as they went. With the help of their old allies the French, the Scots finally forced the English to withdraw, but by this time the Auld Alliance had begun to seem a little burdensome to many in Scotland.

In the 1550s the Reformation reached Scotland, bringing with it a natural alignment with England rather than France from then onwards. After further political chaos, Queen Mary, who had given birth to a son, James, was forced to fly the country, seeking shelter in England with Elizabeth. In the same year, 1567, the infant James VI was proclaimed Scotland's King. There followed a series of regents, with the inevitable plotting and intrigue amongst the nobility, until eventually James himself took over the reins of government. It was a period of economic difficulty. In 1572 there was a severe famine, when the Regent Mar was compelled to encourage emigration by proclamation. Although matters never again reached such a pitch, 1587 was another famine year, as was 1595. At such times many Scots were forced to leave the country and try their fortune elsewhere.

During the latter half of the sixteenth century there was a considerable movement of Lowland Scots into Shetland, specifically to farm the land. The introduction of Scottish bishops to Orkney throughout the previous century and a half had resulted in large numbers of Scots accompanying them as dependants. By the mid-sixteenth century, accordingly, the Norse language had begun to disappear in Orkney, being replaced by Lowland Scots. By the start of the seventeenth century the same process was almost complete in Shetland, though the Isles inevitably retained marks of their long period of Norwegian rule.

Even in the medieval period, between the thirteenth and sixteenth centuries, Scotland's greatest export was undoubtedly men. Scotsmen were travelling abroad even then as merchants, as seamen, frequently as privateers (or plain pirates), as soldiers of fortune (or mercenaries), as scholars and as clerics from travelling friar to bishop. Before the long period of intermittent warfare between England and Scotland initiated by Edward I's invasions, the Scots frequently seem to have settled in England in one or other of these roles. The family of Scott in Dunwich, known variably as le Scot, le Escot, or de Skot, are a good instance of what must have been quite a common occurrence then. They appear to have settled in Dunwich in the twelfth century and by 1260 were long established there. In that year two Hamburg merchants complained that, when passing the coast of Dunwich in a ship laden with corn 'Luke le Scot, Richard le Scot and many others of Dunwich came with boats and attacked the ship and took a large part of the corn contained in her . . .'

Despite the Hamburg merchants' complaints, these early Anglo-Scots, the Scotts of Dunwich, went from strength to strength, becoming mayors and Members of Parliament. It is clear they were far from isolated examples of their kind. Younger sons in large families, reared in a land where they had to work hard merely to scrape a bare existence, needed little prompting to sample life elsewhere.

As merely one example, the name Teit is today still common in Finland. All Teits, it seems, are descended from a certain Jacobus Tait from East Lothian, who was in the service of the Birger Jarl in the mid-thirteenth century. The name James Tait is still common enough in East Lothian and, presumably, those so named could, by Scottish standards at any rate, claim kinship with the Teits in Finland. Other Scottish names well known in Finland today, although probably originating from a much later date such as the Swedish wars of the seventeenth century, are those of Ramsay and Mackay, while the well known Finnish name of Makinnen may well be a corruption of Mackinnon. There are many similar instances where Scottish kinship might be claimed.

The subject of Scottish kinship is one of considerable importance. Family ties, however remote, have always meant a great deal in Scotland and failing ties of kinship by blood or marriage, those of locality have also always meant a great deal. It might be argued that subconsciously this marks a crisis of identity. It might also be claimed that the Scots have always subconsciously felt threatened by their larger and more powerful neighbour in the south, so that to identify with a family or a place has always been important to them, as well as to identify with the Scottish nation. Hence, especially when abroad, the Scots are most aggressively Scottish, needing to assert their origins and hold on to an identity.

Throughout their history, owing to this marked national trait, whenever the Scots nobility were at odds with their king, or with rival nobility, they had little difficulty in recruiting followers. Whether it was a Maxwell or a Johnston in Dumfries, or a Macgregor or Campbell on Loch Lomondside, the principal remained the same. Any large family such as the Douglases, the Gordons, the Hamiltons, the Hepburns, or the Kennedys, to name but a few, could rely on the support of others of their name and their followers. Above all the Scots prized loyalty, whether to an employer, to the head of the family, to a king, or to the nation. With precious little else to offer, they naturally valued highly what they could provide.

It was perhaps for this reason that the Scots proved themselves such notable mercenaries in Europe, particularly in France. As early as the late ninth century, Charles III of France was reputed to have had a Scottish bodyguard. In the mid-thirteenth century a Scottish force fought in the Eighth Crusade under Louis IX. Following the founding of the Auld Alliance in 1295, such service became more frequent. Many Scots served with the French forces in the Hundred Years War, from the mid-fourteenth to the mid-fifteenth centuries. From these were formed the Scottish Archer Guard, Les Gardes du Corps Ecossoises, which was the bodyguard of the King of France, and later the Scottish Men-At-Arms, Les Gens d'Armes Ecossoises, amongst the élite forces in France. It was an honour for Frenchmen to serve in them. Although towards the end of the sixteenth century these had become almost entirely French, they still used the Scots challenges and counters.

Naturally, over the centuries, many Scots settled in France, particularly during the Hundred Years War. The slaughter of the French aristocracy by the English left many vacancies to be filled, either by marriage or as awards for valour. The alterations which names underwent in the process could often be confusing and difficult to follow. In a few generations, with changing titles, Scottish origins were often completely lost and forgotten.

An early example of a Scot acquiring a French title is that of one Nicholas Chambers, or Chambre, who was granted the seigneury of Guerche in Touraine in 1444 by King Charles II.

Not long afterwards the lands of Arcenay in Burgundy were acquired through marriage by one Cunningham, spelled variously Coningans, Conyghan, or Coninglant. Although apparently disappearing at the time of the French Revolution, the family reappeared in 1814 and is said to be still in existence today. Another family established in Burgundy was that of Kinninmond, corrupted into Quinemonts, seigneurs of numerous domains. In the nobility of Touraine, 'La Famille Gohory' is also noted – a corruption of the familiar Scots name Gowrie. Other such corruptions include de Gaulle for Dougal, du Glas for Douglas, Dromont for Drummond, de Crafort for Crawford, D'Handresson for Anderson, D'Espence for Spence, Leviston for Livingstone, de Lisle for Leslie, de Lauzon for Lawson, Locart for Lockhart, Mauricon for Morrison, Montcrif for Moncrieff, Folcart for Flockhart, Torneboule for Turnbull, Le Clerc for Clark, Vullençon for Williamson and de Ramezay for Ramsay.

Apart from the Scottish mercenary, who naturally thrived on wars, another familiar figure overseas was of course the Scottish scholar or cleric. Many Scots studied at Oxford in the thirteenth century, but after prolonged hostilities broke out between Scotland and England, although scholarship supposedly knows no bounds, the Scots mostly gravitated to the continent, notably to the universities at Paris and Orléans. With the Great Schism in the Church of Rome between 1378 and 1417, when the French supported a rival Pope, the Scots were forced to look elsewhere. Some went to Cologne, to the university founded there in 1389, but it was in this educational vacuum that the university of St Andrews was founded in 1411. This was to be followed by Glasgow in 1451, Aberdeen in 1495, and Edinburgh in 1583. Meanwhile Copenhagen university had been founded in 1479. Thus the Scots scholar had a wide choice, both overseas and at home. Despite the Reformation, some 400 Scots appear to have attended the Collège d'Ecosse in Paris University during the sixteenth century.

As is often the case today, not all scholars were content with merely attending one university, and some no doubt attended Paris, Orléans, Cologne, or Copenhagen after first graduating in Scotland. Some stayed abroad for as long as twenty years. Others in holy orders turned to the church, as for example one John Carmichael, or Kirkmichael, who became Bishop of Orléans under the title of Jean de St Michel. Others gravitated to Rome, before the Reformation provided an alternative choice.

France was by no means the only country where the Scots found opportunities for advancement. There was already a thriving Scots community of merchants in the Low Countries, particularly Holland, although their numbers were fairly restricted. During the sixteenth century especially, both Poland and East Prussia were regarded as highly desirable places for the emigrating Scot. There were several causes of emigration at this time: the English invasions of the 1540s, the religious upsets of the 1550s, and the political chaos during and after Queen Mary's reign, were probably reason enough for many, but the stringent economic climate and the famine of 1572, when (as noted) the Regent Mar was compelled to encourage emigration, and the subsequent famines of 1587 and 1595 resulted in numbers of young Scots being forced to leave the country or starve.

The attraction of Poland to many, at least in the early stages, was that there was no middle class between the nobility and the peasants. This was a gap the Scots set about filling with a will. Coming at first mainly from the class of the small laird or town trader, the Scots pedlar with his pack full of woollen goods, cloth, and tin- or iron-ware such as scissors and knives, was soon a familiar sight in Poland. The Scots also kept booths and small shops in the towns and frequently attached themselves to powerful Polish princes, to whom they acted as bankers. As far back as 1531 there is a list of Scots burgesses in Danzig, and throughout the sixteenth century they extended their influence.

Known throughout Poland as 'Kramers or Cramers' (pedlars) they were not, however, all successful by any means. Significantly, the saying 'Poor as a Scot's pedlar's pack' soon became proverbial in Poland and Sir George Skene, writing in 1569, in his dictionary under the word 'pedlar' noted that he had met a great many in poor condition at Cracow; 'many suffered great privations and dangers, and they were not by any means all prosperous'. Fynes Morison writing in 1598 wrote: 'the Scots flocke in greate numbers into Poland, abounding in all thinges for foode ... rather for the poverty of their owne kingdome, than for any great trafficke they exercised there, dealing rather for small fardels, than for great quantities of rich ware.' In the sixteenth century it seems the restrictions on such traders were still fairly fierce, unless they could obtain exemptions for trading but as burgesses of Scottish birth or descent became members of the town guilds, trading for Scots became generally easier.

Meanwhile numbers of Scots had entered mercenary service in Sweden and Denmark, as for instance the brothers William and Hugh Colquhoun, sons of Sir Andrew Colquhoun of Luss, who went to Sweden in the 1560s as officers of a troop of Scottish horse. In Sweden they were called Cahun and as such their family still survives. Similarly the two sons of Johannes Stuart of Ochiltree, who served as Colonel under Francis II of France until 1560, were the first of their name in Sweden, and from 1582 Hans Stuart owned the estate of Hedelunda for 200 years. That family also still survives to this day. There are numerous other instances although many like them failed to perpetuate their name or returned to Scotland.

With the turn of the seventeenth century, Scotland entered into a new era entirely. In 1603 Sir Robert Carey rode up to Holyrood Palace from London in less than three days to inform James of Queen Elizabeth I's death. Two days later the news arrived from the Privy Council that James had been acknowledged her successor. Thus the King of the Scots became also the King of the English; King James VI of Scotland became also King James I of England. Thenceforwards Scotland, the 'antient kingdom', receded steadily into the background and James moved south to London. The first cluster of nobility who went with him was gradually followed by a flood of the more influential and commercially minded; aping the ways of their southern neighbours and forgetting their old independence – forgetting also their old ties with the Continent and gradually losing their individuality.

2

From the union of the Crowns
to 1707

In the thirty years between 1570 and 1600 there had been severe inflation in Scotland, due to debasement of the currency and to the general disorders. In the latter years of the sixteenth century 'beggars and vagrant poor' were reported in 'infinite numbers, and by the same reason of their extreme want and misery, very bold and impudent'. In the early seventeenth century the Venetian ambassador in London noted of Scotland: 'The kingdom itself is populous, the women being prolific, showing how much more fruitful are the northern parts.' All of which probably tended to produce a 'spirit of emigration', for it was often a choice between leaving home or starving. Under the feudal methods of agriculture there was only a limited food supply available, even in good years and when the population increased beyond a certain point, with no plague or famine to check it, the young had little option but seek their fortune, or at least their food, outside Scotland.

By the turn of the seventeenth century, however, Scotland had begun to regain the firm and stable government she had had before Flodden. It had taken almost 100 years to make good the ground lost, but slowly James VI had begun to take over the reins of government. It was not until he had acceded to the English throne that he attained his full powers, but then, acting through a Privy Council appointed in the south, he was able to say with truth that he could 'govern Scotland with my pen; I write and it is done'.

As part of an early policy to 'civilize' the Western Isles and the Highlands, James introduced a system of 'plantations' of 'answerable' (i.e., obedient) Lowlanders. In 1597 an Act was passed to this end and in the autumn of 1599 some 500 or so Lowland settlers were transported to the Isle of Lewis. Three years later those who had not already succumbed to the climate were massacred by the native Islanders. Subsequent similar attempts met with as little success. Somewhat more successful was the Earl of Argyll's foundation of the Burgh of Campbeltown in the Kintyre peninsula with a plantation of Lowlanders. A further plantation of Lowlanders was later also introduced into Inveraray, amongst the first moves to civilize the Highlanders.

In 1603, on James VI and I's accession to the throne of England, the Borders still remained under the system of control by separate Scottish and English Wardens of the Marches, instituted by James IV. They were, however, obviously not proving very effective. In 1602 a law was passed requiring the Scottish nobility and gentry to swear not to protect, consort with, set free, or warn offenders against the law and to agree to the pursuit of fugitives, which in itself indicates the degree of lawlessness still then common.

In 1605 James formed a single commission of five Scots and five Englishmen to control the entire Border region on both sides. There followed a period of intensive and ruthless government such as the region had never known. In 1606 a number of English Grahams, one of the more troublesome English Border families, were transported to Connaught and fifteen Scots were banished, while thirty-two Borderers were executed and 150 were official fugitives. So it went on until eventually James was satisfied that his 'Middle Shires' were at last quiet and peaceful. In practice the effects seem to have been twofold, in that considerable numbers of Borderers were no doubt forced to go overseas at least temporarily 'for the good of their health', while instead of Border reiving, or cattle rustling, those who were so minded turned to smuggling. Although the Crowns were united, excise duties differed, making smuggling a profitable venture; and quantities of spirits, silks and other goods were slipped across the border without benefit to the excise. The Borderers were nothing if not adaptable.

Turning his attention to another trouble-spot, namely Ireland, James conceived the policy of introducing plantations of Scots and English into Ulster. Hitherto the presence of Scots in Ireland would have been considered undesirable, because they were likely to ally with the Irish against the English. With the advent of James VI and I to the English throne the presence of Scots in Ireland became a positive advantage as a source of control over the Irish. Thoroughly despoiled and depopulated during the

Elizabethan wars, Ulster was a natural choice for colonization of this nature.

During the sixteenth century many Scots, mainly Highlanders and Islanders, had gone to Ireland as mercenaries, known as gallowglass. While most of these Scots, having come as soldiers, usually to fight the English with the Irish, had ended as settlers, the Lowland Scots introduced in the plantations were intended as settlers who would be prepared, if necessary, to be soldiers in the event of a rebellion. Before the setting up of the plantations in Ulster, certain Scots were already large landowners there.

The Scottish family of Macdonnell, once Lords of the Isles, had inherited large estates in Antrim through marriage. In 1603 the current chieftain, Sir Randal Macdonnell, was acknowledged as landlord of a vast area of Antrim. The chieftain of County Down, Con O'Neill, was less fortunate, being still in prison for rebellion at Elizabeth's death and James's accession. Two con-niving Scots – an Ayrshire laird, Hugh Montgomery of Braid-stone, a member of James's court who was to become Viscount Airds, and an erstwhile schoolmaster and Scottish agent in Ireland, James Hamilton, who was to become Viscount Clandes-boye – between them shared two-thirds of O'Neill's estates.

George Montgomery, brother of Hugh, who had been a protégé of Elizabeth's in a living in Somerset and had passed news of events to his brother at James's court, was rewarded with the Bishopric of Derry, Raphoe and Clogher. He arrived in 1606 and began to 'plant' the diocesan lands. In the process he became a considerable thorn in the flesh of the Earls of Tyrone and Tyrconnel. In 1607, believing themselves to be in danger of imprisonment, the Earls, with their friends and relations to the number of some sixty, fled to self-appointed exile. With their flight their lands were forfeit to the Crown. In 1609 the Crown invited 'undertakers' to take up their share in the proposed plantations in Ulster. There were numerous applicants, but ultimately fifty-nine undertakers were chosen and allocated 81,000 acres of land between them.

From 1610 onwards the first Lowlanders and their families settled in the lands provided for them in Ulster. Almost at once, however, a new problem arose in that some of those outlawed by the Border Commission promptly fled to Ulster. Furthermore they frequently took with them cattle and horses stolen in the

Lowlands or Borders, which met with a ready sale on the Irish side of the channel where they were, of course, much in demand by the new settlers.

A Proclamation issued in 1611 by the Scottish Council read in part: 'This thievish and wicked trade has had such a course and progres this yeir begane as now is become most frequent and common.' As already noted, the Borderers were ready to turn their hand to any opportunity that arose and this variant on an old theme must have seemed heaven-sent.

A typical case was noted in 1612, when the Scottish Privy Council granted a commission for the arrest of a certain John Hislop, who, it was stated, had for the past two years taken a number of stolen horses from Scotland to Ireland and was said to have just returned for a fresh shipment. Such traffic was clearly extremely hard to control. The captains of vessels employed in ferrying men and beasts between the two countries were themselves, almost certainly, taking a share in the profits, if not directly related to the horse and cattle thieves, or involved with them in other smuggling ventures.

In 1616 the Scottish Privy Council took drastic action, dividing the west coast into four sections, in each of which special ports were assigned to handle the Irish traffic. An elaborate passport system was introduced and two commissioners were appointed to supervise the entire system. Unfortunately the Irish themselves never instituted similar controls so that this was a one-sided operation and, not unnaturally, by 1622 it had broken down completely. By this time it appears to have become as profitable to steal cattle and horses in Ulster and ship them to Scotland as the reverse had been earlier. Many a Borderer, it was noted, now arrived in Ulster on foot and returned to Scotland with three or four horses.

In 1622 the Irish council issued a proclamation deploring the number of Scots 'of the meaner sort' who it noted as being 'much more abounding here than in former times'. It was proposed that all wandering Scots who could not account for themselves should be gaoled until they could prove that they had no criminal record. Unfortunately like many Irish edicts it appears never to have been put into effect, which was probably a sign of the general stagnation that seems to have overtaken Ulster in the later years of James's reign.

One of the possible reasons for this stagnation may have been that the Scots had found other outlets for their surplus population and energies. As early as 1616 William Lithgow, the noted Scots traveller, termed Poland the 'mother and nurse of the youths and younglings of Scotland, clothing, feeding and enriching them with the fatness of her best things, besides 30,000 Scots families that live incorporate in her bowels'. Whether that figure was anything like accurate or not, there can be no question that there were very many Scots resident in Poland and that too many youngsters unable to look after themselves properly resorted to begging, or theft, giving the others a bad name. Patrick Gordon, the Scottish consul in Danzig, drew the King's attention to this and pointed out that the Scottish settlers in Poland themselves wished some check put on the emigrants.

In 1625, therefore, the King issued a proclamation.

Whereas the grite number of young boyes uncapable of service and destitute of meanis liveing yearlie transported out of that our kingdome to the East-seas and specially to the town of Dantzik and there manie tymes miserable in grite numbers dyeing in the streets have given quite scandall to the people of those countries and laid one foull imputation on that our kingdome, to the grite hinderance and detriment of those our subjects of the better, who traffique in the saidis countreyis; it is our pleasour, that by oppin proclamatioun ye cause prohibite all maisters of shippes to transport anie youthes of either sex to the said easterne countreyis bot such as either salbe sent by their friends dwelling there, or then, sall carrie with them sufficient meanis of maintenance at least for ane yeare under the pane of fyfe hundred markis monie of that our kingdome, toties quoties they sall offend in that kind.

Whether this had much effect is open to question, but it is indicative of the size of the problem. Some of the corruptions of Scottish names which arose in Poland and East Prussia at this time are of interest since no doubt they were perpetuated and many Poles and Germans to this day may not appreciate that they have Scottish blood. In Warsaw some typical corruptions noted in various documents were Chalmers to Czamer, Drew to Driow-sky, Weir to Wier, Soutar to Zutter, Scott to Zlot, Brown to Burn,

Macallan to Makalienski, Wright to Rytt, Graem to Grim, Carmichael to Larmche, Moir to Mora, Ross to Rusek. In Prussia the corruptions noted were Arnott to Ahrnett, Auld to Altt, Polwarth to Bollwarth, Brown to Bruin, Bruce to Bruisz, Forbes to Ferbrus, Douglas to Doglass, Duncan to Duncken, Archibald to Etzbald, Cockburn to Kaubrun, Cumming to Koning, Hendry to Heinrich, McCall to Magall, Nichol to Nickel, Scott to Schotte, Wright to Wricht. There were, of course, very many more.

The outbreak of the Thirty Years War in 1618 saw many Scots enlist as mercenaries, especially under Gustavus Adolphus in Sweden. At one time it was estimated that some 10,000 were serving in Sweden and this included no less than three field marshals, fourteen generals of varying degree, forty-one colonels (including eight Leslies, seven Hamiltons and two Lumsdens) twenty captains (including four Mackays and three Stewarts), as well as numerous others.

One of the more prominent figures behind much of the Scottish enlistment in Sweden at this time was Sir James Spens of Wormiston, who acted as ambassador in Sweden for James VI and I. In 1623 his son James enlisted 1,200 Scots for service against Poland. After long and valuable service as ambassador, he died in Sweden and his descendants are prominent there to-day.

Three other examples, amongst many, of Scottish founders of families in Scandinavia, which have lasted to the present day are of interest. As already noted in the 1560s William and Hugh Colquhoun, sons of Sir Alexander Colquhoun of Luss, went to Sweden as officers of a troop of Scottish horse, and as Cahun their descendants are still flourishing. In the year 1573, James Ramsay of Dalhousie settled in Sweden: his son, Captain Hans Ramsay of Dalhousie, was enobled in 1633 and his Swedish-Finnish descendants included Carl Henrik Ramsay, Foreign Minister of Finland in 1945. Robert Douglas, younger son of Patrick Douglas of Standingstone, the younger son of William Douglas of Whittingehame, went to Sweden in 1627 as a trooper, rose to Lieutenant Colonel in 1634, General and Baron Skalby in 1651, Count of Skanninge in 1654, ultimately becoming Field Marshal in 1657 and Commander-in-Chief from 1658 –1660, dying in Stockholm in 1661. A descendant of his was Commander-in-Chief of the Swedish Army in the Second World War.

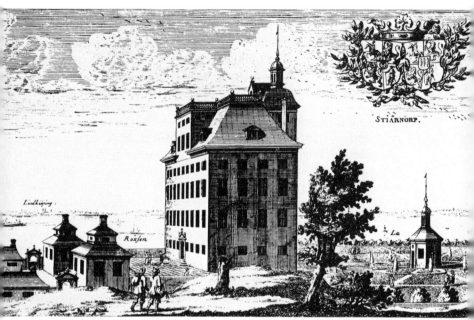

The manor Stjärnorp, built by Robert Douglas who left Scotland for Sweden in 1627, and prospered there: detail of an engraving printed in the late seventeenth century.

The principal reasons for emigration were, until the later stages of James's reign, undoubtedly economic: those who saw no chance of improving their lot in Scotland, and a very real chance of starving if they stayed, quickly decided to leave. It was not until the last years of his reign that religion began to be an issue of any real importance. In the years after 1620, however, James sowed the seeds of religious differences which were to rend Scotland for the greater part of the seventeenth century.

By dint of packing the Perth Assembly of 1618 with his supporters, he achieved his desire to make Scottish religious ceremonies conform with those of the English. In 1621 the Five Articles of Perth were ratified by the Scottish Parliament. Only then did the Scots find their methods of worship seriously affected, and the power given to the bishops was the principal bone of contention. It was this that formed the basis of almost all the subsequent religious dissension in Scotland.

About the same period the Scots began to be attracted by the new world opening in the west. In 1621 Sir William Alexander, a favourite of James's who was created Earl of Stirling nine years later, was given vast tracts of land in Cape Breton, Prince Edward Island, and New Brunswick, as well as parts of Vermont, New Hampshire, Maine and Quebec. With the idea of founding a New Scotland, like the New England and New Holland already founded, he attempted to form a settlement in Nova Scotia. The first settlers left Scotland in 1622 and arrived in Nova Scotia in the autumn. They survived the winter with some losses and were relieved by a second ship in 1623, but nothing was achieved in the way of permanent settlement.

In 1625 Alexander obtained the King's agreement to the creation of the famous Nova Scotia Baronetcies. By this scheme any Scottish gentleman agreeing to provide a number of settlers and a sum amounting to £166 could become a 'Baronet of Nova Scotia'. For this purpose, part of the Castlehill in front of Edinburgh Castle, now the Esplanade, was declared Nova Scotian territory, so that the newly created baronets could take physical possession of their American estates without ever actually leaving Scotland. In the end, the obligation to provide men was scrapped and payment of a further sum in lieu was substituted. In all, sixty-four baronets were created, the first being Sir Robert Gordon in 1625. In the circumstances, not unnaturally, a suspicion arose that the entire scheme was merely a confidence trick to benefit the chronically ailing finances of Sir William Alexander.

With the outbreak of war between England and France in 1627, the Scots operating against the French in Canada, led by the Kirke brothers, captured Port Royal, and in 1629 Quebec also, where Captain David Kirke appointed his brother Captain Louis Kirke governor. In 1629 and 1631 a number of Scottish settlers arrived in Port Royal, but Charles I, perennially short of funds, ordered the abandonment of the settlement in return for a suitable financial payment. Thus Nova Scotia remained in French hands for a further sixty-two years before finally being settled by the Scots.

One other attempt was made at the same time to settle in the area, when Lord Ochiltree landed some settlers in Cape Breton in 1629. Not strong enough to withstand the attacks of the French, they were driven out after only a few months and Cape

Breton remained under French sovereignty for a further 134 years. It is interesting to speculate whether any of the Scots fighting for the English at that time encountered fellow Scots, or their descendants, fighting for the French. This had occurred frequently during fighting in Europe, but the only apparent record of a Scot staying behind when the Kirkes abandoned Quebec is of a certain Abraham Martin, *'dit l'Ecossais'*.

Thus the first venture into Nova Scotia by the Scots merely resulted in the creation of sixty-four baronetcies, many of which are still in existence, but in no permanent settlement. Apart from the suggestion in 1635 by Sir William Alexander, by then the Earl of Stirling, that a Scottish 'plantation' should be made in Maine amidst a settlement already founded by the English, nothing further was done about promoting Scottish settlements in North America for the time being. It was significant, however, that the next Scottish settlements did in fact take this shape, being plantations of Scots in predominantly English settlements.

Meanwhile, in Ulster official inaction and inefficiency were sowing the seeds of future trouble. Sir George Hamilton of Greenlaw, like his father Lord Hamilton, was a Roman Catholic. On the death of his brothers Sir George ultimately inherited control of a large portion of Strabane. Through his influence many of his neighbours, including the young Earl of Abercorn, also turned to Roman Catholicism. As early as 1614 the authorities knew of Sir George's religious beliefs, and instructions were issued that he must either conform or be expelled; but, as so often in Ireland, nothing was done. By 1622, there were already claims of discrimination against Presbyterians in the Strabane area. By 1630 the Bishop of Derry warned that if matters were not controlled there would be a rebellion in Strabane.

It was, in fact, in Scotland that religious unrest first arose. In 1631, eight years after his accession, Charles I was crowned in Scotland and the religious differences between the Scots and their Stuart kings came to a head. Unlike his father, who had at least outwardly employed the legal procedures of Parliament and the General Assembly, Charles attempted to dispense with both. He then appeared surprised at the vehement reaction of the Scots. In 1638 a National Covenant was signed, demanding a free Parliament and a free Assembly. The Scottish reaction was almost spontaneous – meeting in the same year, the Assembly put an end to bishops, to the Five Articles of Perth, and to the new liturgy introduced by Charles I. In short, it replaced Episcopacy with Presbyterianism.

When Charles I remained intransigent, Scotland rose in revolt and the first Bishops' War followed in 1639. It was a bloodless affair and the results were indecisive, so that a second Bishops' War resulted the following year. It too was a bloodless confrontation, since Charles could not raise an army willing to fight for him with enthusiasm. The King then accepted the Covenanters' demands, although this was clearly a case of expediency on his part. However the Covenanters were now split into two parties, one supporting the King and the others opposed to him. The principal protagonists on either side were the Marquis of Montrose for the King and the Marquis of Argyll for the Covenanters.

The First Civil War was fought from 1642 to 1646. In 1644 the Marquis of Montrose, as the King's Lieutenant, raised an army in Scotland composed partly of Irish mercenaries and partly of Highlanders. Although greatly outnumbered, he had the advantage of superior mobility and, using the tactics developed by Gustavus Adolphus, he fought a series of brilliant battles in a campaign lasting a year. Although everywhere triumphant, Montrose's victories had one unfortunate side-effect: they increased the fear and distrust the Lowlanders felt for the Highlanders.

Montrose's brief but brilliant campaign ended in disaster when his army was surprised by a superior force under General Leslie and routed at the battle of Philiphaugh. For the rest of 1645 and part of 1646, Montrose tried to raise another army against the Covenanters, but without success. In 1646, Charles himself joined the Covenanters and ordered Montrose to surrender. In 1647 Charles was handed over to the English at Oliver Cromwell's demand, and in 1648 the Cromwellian forces took control of England, declaring it a Commonwealth, with Cromwell as Protector. In the same year Cromwell's forces defeated a Scottish army at Preston, and in 1649 Charles I was beheaded.

The Scots then declared Charles II King and in 1650 Cromwell invaded Scotland with 16,000 battle-hardened troops. Against these, Leslie raised some 22,000 partly trained recruits, then – by using the scorched-earth policy familiar to the Scots since the time of Edward I, and refusing combat – he successfully thwarted Cromwell, finally forcing him to withdraw to Dunbar.

Unfortunately at the Battle of Dunbar, when it came to actual combat at last, the English routed the Scots with such ease that it became known as the Dunbar Drove.

About 10,000 prisoners were taken and a number of these were finally sold as bond-servants in the colonies. The majority, around 900, went to Virginia and some 150 to New England. The following year to the day, another Scottish army was defeated at the decisive Battle of Worcester, and again many of the prisoners taken were sent overseas to the plantations as bond-servants. Some 1,300 went to Guinea, and about 270 to Boston. During the Scottish uprising against Cromwell's rule in 1653–4, further prisoners were taken, some being sent to the newly acquired island of Jamaica.

Amongst the Scots taken prisoner at the Battle of Worcester were David Ross, twelfth Chief of Balnagowan, and the survivors of his regiment. Some of these were sent to Boston and settled down in that area. On the records there the name Ross appears a number of times from 1654 onwards, when James Ross of Sudbury was the first to be recorded. From that one name alone, more than 2,000 descendants have been traced over the centuries. Many of the present-day Rosses in Massachusetts can trace their ancestry back to these original prisoners sent out by Cromwell. It is not altogether surprising that in 1657 a Scots Charitable Society was founded in Boston with a membership of fifty-seven, the first of its kind to be recorded in America.

Rather than remain in Scotland under the Commonwealth some Scots found it desirable for their health to take up arms as mercenaries on the continent. Prominent amongst these was General Thomas Dalyell of the Binns, who escaped from the Tower in 1651 after being captured at the Battle of Worcester. On joining the Russian army under Tsar Michaelovitch, his first task was to introduce order and discipline. He was so successful that he soon attained the rank of general, but in 1665 at the request of Charles II he obtained leave to return to Scotland, where he was later prominent in the persecution of the Covenanters.

Another Scot with a similar background and career was Patrick Gordon of Auchleuchries in Aberdeenshire. An ardent supporter of the Stuarts, he fled the country to serve as a mercenary in Europe before finally joining the Russian army in 1661, when he was well received by Tsar Alexis. Promoted to general in 1687, he was the power behind the youthful Tsar Peter (Peter the Great). It is significant of the way Scot attracted Scot that in 1690 his daughter Mary married one David Crawfurd also serving in the Russian army. When General Gordon died in 1699, at the age of sixty-four, he was immensely wealthy and powerful as well as being a personal friend of the Tsar.

Somewhat ironically the Scots enjoyed firmer and fairer government during the Commonwealth, with more freedom of trade and less religious bias, than they ever had received under the Stuarts. It was only with the Restoration in 1660, and the return of Charles II, that the Scots once again began to experience religious intolerance and restrictions on trading. From 1665 onwards the Scots followed the example of the English by transporting 'idle' beggars, gipsies and criminals to Virginia, Barbados, and Jamaica, continuing the practice until the end of the century. After the first decade of Charles II's reign, until the Revolution of 1688, the persecution of the Covenanters also developed to the stage where for the first time there was considerable emigration, both voluntary and involuntary, for religious reasons.

Initially, at least, the majority of persecuted Presbyterians chose to join their fellow churchmen in the Scottish colony in Holland, where there were already many Scots. Some, like the Reverend George Turnbull, subsequently a Presbyterian minister for fifty-seven years, spent their time studying for the ministry at the University of Utrecht, worshipping at the Scots church in Rotterdam, and preaching occasionally in Delft. In the company of his father and uncle, Turnbull no doubt found life enjoyable enough, but when news of the Revolution reached him he returned home at once.

In the nature of things, however, a considerable number of Scots must have filtered over to Ireland, where despite the fact that Episcopacy was supposedly the universal faith, both Roman Catholicism and Presbyterianism were flourishing. Between 1609 and 1639 some 40,000 Scots were estimated to have settled in Ulster, but by the 1690s it was estimated that the figure was nearer to a 100,000. In many respects therefore this could be considered amongst the most successful of the Scottish attempts at colonization. The names of those who settled include a large proportion of typical Border and Lowland Scots origin. Elliot,

Armstrong, Scott, Stewart, Cunningham, Irvine, Montgomery, Johnston, Graham, Bell, and Hamilton are perhaps the most common.

In the Highlands, Charles II introduced new measures. Since 1624, Independent Companies consisting solely of Highlanders had been raised as a form of police-force to keep the peace. This had not always worked well in practice, since too often they were prepared to turn a blind eye to transgressions in return for a share of the proceeds. It was also likely that clan loyalties prevented them taking any action when members of their own, or friendly, clans were involved.

On 3 August 1667, Charles issued, under the Great Seal, a commission to the Earl of Atholl to raise and keep such a number of men as he should think fit 'to be a constant guard for ensuring the peace of the Highlands' and 'to watch upon the braes', his jurisdiction to extend to 'the shyres of Inverness, Nairn, Murray, Banff, Aberdeen, Mairnes, Angus, Perth, Clackmannan, Monteith, Stirling and Dumbarton'. His prison, where malefactors might be incarcerated, was to be the Blair of Athol. From this fairly comprehensive commission the very numerous Highland regiments, which were to become famous throughout the world, all stemmed in due course, but at this stage they were merely considered as a means of keeping the peace in the Highlands themselves, for in the south the Highlanders were still considered a lawless and dangerous people.

In 1678 the Earl of Lauderdale raised 6,000 armed Highlanders and marched them down to Ayrshire where the Covenanters were most militant, billeting them there for a month. The 'Highland Host', as it was termed, merely stengthened ill-feeling between Highlander and Lowlander and did nothing to improve the religious situation. The Covenanters did not at first rise against this persecution, as Lauderdale had hoped, so that he was unable to treat them as rebels, although no doubt a number were inclined to slip over to Ulster in the face of such provocation. After the rising in 1679 and the Battle of Bothwell Brig, however, many were deported willy-nilly. One ship carrying 200 was wrecked in Orkney.

From 1638 onwards, East New Jersey was another possible choice for emigrants from Scotland. Controlled by twenty-four proprietors, of whom five were Scots, two Irish, sixteen English and one Dutch (a man who, against all the current trends of the times, lived in Scotland), Scottish emigration was encouraged. In 1684 two ships from Scotland delivered a total of 290 emigrants, most of whom appear to have been fairly solid citizens. They reported back favourably and further emigrants followed. In 1702 New Jersey, by this time flourishing, became a Crown Colony with a good Scottish flavour to it.

Very much less successful was a settlement in South Carolina in the year 1684, mainly composed of Covenanting refugees from persecution. Led by the Reverend William Dunlop, a Presbyterian minister, and Lord Cardross, they moved into Stuart's Town, but their settlement did not last long. In 1686 it was attacked by the Spanish who also laid claim to the area, and was destroyed.

In the meantime several Scots, or descendants of Scots, were making their mark with the French in North America. The most notable at this time would appear to be Claude de Ramezay, undoubtedly of Scots origin, who went to Acadia in 1685 as an ensign of marines and ended up as Governor of Montreal in 1704. Less noteworthy, but of interest in their quieter way, were the Melansons, who appear to have descended from some Scots settlers of that name who settled in Port Royal in 1628 after the Kirke brothers had taken the fort from the French. They apparently remained after the settlement was ceded to the French in 1632, for two brothers Melanson were recorded in Port Royal in 1686. Later the name became quite common as their descendants multiplied.

While under the Commonwealth, as has been noted, there was no discrimination against the Scots and Scotland was well governed, from the Restoration onwards the Scots were much less favoured in many ways than the English. With the return of the Stuarts, Scotland became again the 'ancient kingdome' in the north, never visited, governed from afar, regarded again as a burden rather than an equal partner. For example the English merchants, jealous of their Scottish counterparts, campaigned successfully for trading monopolies with the colonies abroad, both in the west and the east, so that those Scots without considerable influence in the south were unable to obtain licences to trade.

Understandably, Scotland was suffering from a steady drain of nobility and merchants to London. In addition, the old craftsmen of Scotland were already, in many instances, being ignored by the nobility, who, rather than patronize them and continue to use local products, were increasingly importing English fashions from the south. Forced into imitation, the craftsmen lost their own individual styles. Trade with the Continent was also affected, especially with France – once the old ally but now no longer prepared to waive taxes or customs imposts.

The reign of James II and VII was marked by even greater religious intolerance than had been shown in the latter years of Charles II. In 1688, after an ill-fated attempt to reintroduce Roman Catholicism, James was forced to fly the country and take refuge in France, while his daughter Mary and her husband William of Orange were invited to take his place. Although on the accession of William and Mary Presbyterianism at last replaced Episcopacy in Scotland, there was no marked improvement in economic matters.

The brief attempt by Graham of Claverhouse, Earl of Dundee, to emulate Montrose in 1689 and raise a Highland force to conquer all Scotland, ended with his death at Killiecrankie, but once again the Lowlands had been made conscious of the dangers of armed Highlanders under the control of a competent general. Further distrust between Highlander and Lowlander was fostered by the notorious Massacre of Glencoe in 1692 when a force of government soldiers led by a Campbell, was billeted on the Macdonalds of Glencoe and attacked their hosts at a given signal. This was done as the result of an order signed by William, who became in consequence the most despised and hated man in the Highlands.

If the Highlanders distrusted the Lowlanders, some conception of the distorted views of the Highlanders commonly held in the Lowlands may be seen in an extract from a *History of the Revolution in Scotland*, printed in Edinburgh in 1690. This reads:

> The Highlanders of Scotland are the sort of wretches that have no consideration of honour, friendship, obedience or government, than as, by alteration in affairs or revolution in the government, they can improve to themselves an opportunity of robbing or plundering their neighbours.

In the 1690s another major event was the failure of the Darien expedition. This affected more particularly the Lowlands, although the repercussions were felt throughout Scotland. Backed by William Paterson, a Scot who had made a fortune in Jamaica and had founded the Bank of England, the Scots formed 'The Company of Scotland trading in Africa and the Indies' with a view to gaining their share of world markets and trade. The project proposed by Paterson was that of forming a Scottish settlement in the Isthmus of Darien, or Panama. With trade seemingly feasible from there in all directions, it appeared on the face of it an ideal place and William III gave his assent by granting a Crown Charter. Initially there was also considerable English support, until the powerful East India Company made its opposition felt on the grounds that its trade might be adversely affected. The English then withdrew their support, but throughout Scotland support came from every quarter.

In 1698, three ships set out from Leith backed by the hopes and finances of thousands of Scots. Disease, Spanish armed opposition, and lack of any support from the English in North America, caused the total failure of the venture. In the end some 4,000 men were lost and many thousands more back in Scotland were ruined. The Scots understandably blamed the pusillanimous behaviour of both William III and the English.

As early as 1620 some of the leading Glasgow merchants had invested in a Newfoundland Company, which seemed to promise a loophole in the Colonial customs system. By the 1660s, under cover of investing in the Newfoundland fisheries, they were effectively avoiding the customs stranglehold of the English. By 1680 the Surveyor General of the Customs for the American Plantations was complaining that ships laden with tobacco were claiming in Boston to be bound for Newfoundland, when in fact they sailed direct to Glasgow. Another method of evading customs was to register ships in Whitehaven, over the Solway Firth in Cumberland, or alternatively to ship goods to Newfoundland in colonial vessels and thence by Scottish ships direct to the Clyde.

Long before 1707 the Scots were almost openly flouting the customs laws by opening ostensible fishing stations in Newfoundland, which were merely transhipping points for tobacco from Virginia, sugar from the West Indies, and furs and skins from the north. These then went direct to Scotland or Europe. The return trade, in French silks, lace, and brandy to the Colonies, was almost a *sine qua non*, and, since the Scots had a very understandable contempt for the English customs laws, no duty was paid on this trade either. By the turn of the century, indeed, anti-English feeling in Scotland was very high. The Scots were once again close to demanding separation and complete independence.

With the accession of Queen Anne, daughter of James II and VII, in 1702, the situation was not improved, but the union of the Parliaments took place in 1707, despite very strong opposition from many quarters in Scotland. Thereafter Scotland's ability to take any separate action had passed. The nation's future now lay with England in the British colonies abroad. Scotland expanded in the Far East and West, but no longer on her own initiative. For all that, she implanted her genes throughout the world with considerable effect.

3

From the union of
the Parliaments to 1775

At the time of the union of the Parliaments in 1707, Scotland had an estimated population of around a million, of which about 300,000 were Highlanders. There were, it was also estimated, about 100,000 Scots in Ulster, and if a similar growth rate is allowed for Sweden, Poland and elsewhere on the Continent, there must have been approximately 100,000 in Europe and Scandinavia. Some sixty-five years later the estimated number in North America was 150,000, so it would not be unreasonable to put the figure there in 1707 at around 50,000. The total number of emigrant Scots at this time, discounting the very considerable number in England, must therefore have been around a quarter of the total population in Scotland. From this stage onwards the number of Scots emigrating was to grow progressively, while the number remaining in Scotland remained relatively static.

In one respect, and a very important one, Scotland was a long way ahead of England. By the standards of the day, education in Scotland was extremely advanced compared with that of any other country, although otherwise she had few advantages over her wealthier and more powerful neighbour in the south. Backed by Scottish industry, ability, and determination, however, this was sufficient in many ways to tip the balance in favour of the poorer country. In an agricultural economy, for instance, it was very apparent that throughout the eighteenth century Lowland Scotland's farming methods steadily improved, until by 1800 new methods were being developed in the north and sent south to England reversing the previous trend.

In the Highlands things were very different. The romantic view of the Highlanders as noble clansmen devoted to their chiefs, who in turn cared for them and looked after them, owes much to Sir Walter Scott. In reality, cut off by lack of communication, often suffering from inbreeding with its attendant evils, and still existing under a feudal system requiring military service at the chief's command, the Highlanders lived a precarious life, with barely enough to eat and with no chance of relief in times of famine. Underclad and at the mercy of the elements, the High-landers lived in turf-roofed, earth-floored hovels, scarcely worthy of the name of huts, without windows or chimneys, permeated by peat-smoke.

Captain Burt, an engineer officer working on the roads in the Highlands under General Wade, noted the amazing quantities of whisky drunk. He recorded: '. . . usky . . . though a strong spirit, is to them like water. And this I have often seen them drink out of a scallop shell.' Drunk in this fashion, almost straight from the primitive stills, it must have been a raw spirit indeed, but it probably provided some slight relief from a life of poverty, as well as a protection against the climate.

The women, starting young, might bear as many as twenty children who were highly susceptible to periodic attacks of smallpox. They worked hard in the tiny fields, using a wooden plough and other primitive tools, as well as weaving in their houses. The men, paying their rent to the tacksmen (middle-men between them and their chief) and liable to military service at the chief's call, were little better off. Yet, unlike the Lowlanders, they felt no urge to work and much of their time was spent making music, singing, drinking, and sheltering from the abysmal weather, which often made work impossible.

The old method of land-leasing in the Highlands consisted of the chieftain gránting to close relatives leases, or tacks, of large areas of land at token rents; in return they provided, when required, a given number of men for military service. The tacksman then sublet his land in smaller lots to groups who farmed in common, paying rent and giving military service as and when required. As the need for military service decreased and finally lapsed, so the need for the tacksman also passed. Once the chieftain became the direct landlord, inevitably his relationship with his clansmen also changed.

In one important respect the Highlands had been slowly developing in the latter part of the seventeenth century. Many younger sons of chieftains and tacksmen had been educated in the Scottish universities and many clansmen already had relations well placed in offices as merchants and lawyers in Edinburgh and elsewhere. With the emergence of Glasgow as an important port for tobacco merchants in the eighteenth century, there was inevitably a close link there with the Highlands.

There was, however, still deep distrust of the Lowlands and of the southern government. Partly this was based on religion, for prior to 1715 the clans, apart from the Campbells, had predominantly Roman Catholic, or Episcopalian, rather than Presbyterian, sympathies. It was only in the eighteenth century, at the instigation of the Society for the Propagation of Christian Knowledge, that ministers were sent from the Lowlands to instil the Presbyterian faith in the Highlands.

One of these ministers' duties was to teach the Highlanders English and 'root out the Erse language'. To be fair, such instructions went back to the time of James VI and I, who had first instituted the idea of enforced education in English for the sons of the chieftains of the Western Isles. It was not, however, until after the rebellion of 1715 that the impact of these ministers began to be felt.

With the union, the Scots had been given the promise of freedom to practise Presbyterianism as the religion of Scotland and allowed to continue to use their own legal system. They were also free to trade within the developing Empire, a clause of which they made full and immediate use. Having only forty-eight members in the House of Commons, and sixteen in the House of Lords, they had little or no influence on events, more especially in those days when government was conducted largely through powerful blocs or cabals, organized by means of rotten boroughs and the open buying of seats. To all intents and purposes from this point onwards, Scotland was merely an appendage of England. Despite this the Scots had a great deal to offer the Empire, and the contribution of those who went abroad was out of all proportion to their numbers.

The death of Queen Anne, however, found Scotland still only very uneasily united with England. There were many Scots, both in the Lowlands and the Highlands, who did not approve of the idea of the union of the Parliaments and who were prepared to stomach Episcopalianism, or even Roman Catholicism, with a return to the Stuarts, rather than suffer continued rule by the Hanoverian, German-speaking, George I, who was advised almost exclusively by Englishmen. Had James VII and II and his Jacobite supporters in Scotland acted more promptly and decisively, it is quite possible that the rebellion of 1715, so tardily and half-heartedly started by the Earl of Mar, might have succeeded.

The false notion that after the 1715 rebellion great numbers of Scots prisoners were sent to the plantations in North America is one that still persists. Although some were indeed condemned as bond-servants to the plantations in Virginia, Maryland, South Carolina, and Antigua, the total does not seem to have exceeded 800, of whom some may well have escaped and returned before their time expired, or may never even have departed at all.

In any event, there is good reason to suppose that quite a number of these Highlanders considered themselves well placed when they finally arrived in the plantations. A letter printed in the *Maryland Historical Magazine* was dictated by a certain Donald Macpherson in 1717 from Maryland to his father in Inverness-shire and was apparently written down by a friend from Glasgow. The result, written in Lowland Scots with a phonetic translation of Highland speech, is a very strange epistle. It reads:

> My Mestire says til me, Fan I kan speek lyk de Fouk hier dat I sanna pi pidden di nating pat gar his Plackimores wurk; for desyt Fouk hier dinna ise to wurk pat de first Yeer after tey kum in te de Quintry; Tey speak a lyke de Sogers in Inerness.

The translation of this verbatim message is plain enough to anyone accustomed to Lowland Scots and to the Highland methods of pronunciation:

> My Master says to me, when I can speak like the folk here that I shall not be bidden to do nothing but make his blackamoors work; for decent folk here do not use to work but the first year after they come into the country; they speak all like the soldiers in Inverness.

Donald Macpherson obviously did not seem unduly concerned at his deportation and he was certainly amongst a minority of Jacobite prisoners dealt with in this way. Writing less than a decade later, Daniel Defoe noted: 'So many of the Scots servants which go over to Virginia settle and thrive there, than of the English . . . that if it goes on for many years more, Virginia may be rather called a Scots than an English plantation.' Already it seems as if some Scots at least were beginning to regard transportation not so much as a punishment but as a positive advantage.

The general reaction to the rebellion of 1715 indicates, as clearly as anything, the extent of Jacobite sympathies at the time. Although a Disarming Act was passed forbidding the carrying of arms in the Highlands, little was done to enforce it. It was not until 1725 and afterwards, when the Irish General George Wade had set about building his military roads through the Highlands, that anything effective could be done to enforce such Acts.

Meanwhile in 1721 London had a Scotsman, Sir William Stewart, as Lord Mayor. Increasingly Scottish merchants and bankers were gaining control of business in the City of London. Nor was this influence restricted to London. In 1720 a Scotsman named James Macrae, an able ship's captain who had successfully disposed of a number of pirate vessels, entered the East India Company's service. In 1725 he was appointed Governor of Madras, finally returning home as one of the earliest Scottish nabobs (a derogatory form of the Indian title 'Nawab') with a handsome fortune in 1740. In North Carolina the first Governor was William Drummond, a Lowlander, and another, Thomas Pollock, was one of the first members of the Council. In Virginia, James Blair was acting as Commissary, later rising to Governor, but already being accused of favouring his fellow Scots. This indeed was a charge, difficult to deny since often true, which was to be made against many Scots in high office overseas.

In the Highlands, General George Wade set about his task of building military roads by raising in 1725 six Independent Companies under Lord Lovat. Sir Duncan Campbell of Lochnell, and Colonel William Grant of Ballindalloch, who held the rank of captains. Each Company consisted of some 500 men, recruited with the intention of preventing theft and disorder and of enforcing the Disarming Acts. It was at this time that the 'Government' Black Watch tartan was evolved. The majority of the Highlanders recruited for these forces were from the Presbyterian and Whig clans of Campbell, Grant, and Fraser.

In 1727 George II succeeded his father, like him unable to speak more than indifferent broken English with a guttural German accent. In 1732 the settlement of Georgia was founded, and in the same year James Innes from Caithness, and Hugh

Campbell and William Forbes, all took grants of land in the Cape Fear River area of North Carolina. The first of many Highlanders to settle in that region, they soon prospered. In 1734 James Innes was appointed a Justice of the Peace, and in the same year Gabriel Johnston, another Scot, took up the office of Governor of North Carolina. Working in close co-operation, they were to encourage many Scots, particularly Highlanders, to emigrate to that region.

Between 1726 and the late 1730s General Wade continued with his road-building in the Highlands. At the same time he built three strategically placed forts along the line of the Great Glen, namely Fort William on Loch Linnhe in the south-west, Fort Augustus at the foot of Loch Ness in the centre and Fort George, above Inverness. The object of these, of course, was to keep the Highlanders penned in the west should they again rebel. In practice, once the Highlands had been opened up to travellers by the building of the military roads, the forts themselves were superfluous, but the principles employed in the colonial plantations to repel Red Indians were clearly being employed in this instance. The parallel between the treatment of the Indians and of the Highlanders is striking.

In 1739 a group of Highlanders from Argyll, numbering 350 and made up of some eighty-five to ninety families under the leadership of 'Duncan Campbell, Dugald MacNeal, Daniel MacNeal, Colonel MacAlister and Neal MacNeal', arrived in the Cape Fear region of North Carolina. They were the first to settle in the Cross Creek district of Cape Fear, where subsequently many more were to follow. It was also one of the earlier parties in this area to be led by men of substance, presumably tacksmen. This was a pattern which followed the 1745 rebellion, continuing up to 1775, as the tacksmen began to find their rents rising owing to the fact that chieftains no longer required men for military service in lieu of rent.

In the following year, 1740, land grants registered included ten to Duncan Campbell, four to James McLachlan, four to Daniel McNeil, four to Neil McNeil, two to Archibald Douglass, one to Colonel Macalister, one to James Macalister, one each to Patrick Stewart and Douglas Stewart, also single grants to James Campbell, Archibald McGill, James Fergus, James McDugald, Hugh McCraine, Gilbert Pattison, Jno McFerson, Murdoch McBraine and Alex McKay. Only one of these land grants was for less than

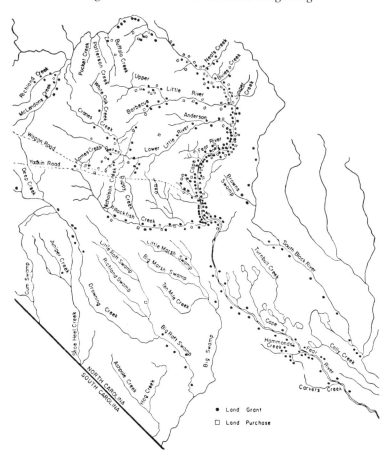

Land grants and purchases of land made by Highlanders in North Carolina, 1733–1765.

100 acres and the eight largest were for 640 acres apiece, the average being 320 acres. Clearly most of them were for the benefit of several families, being sub-let to them in individual plots.

To a greater degree than most Scottish emigrants, Highlanders tended to remain in the area to which they first emigrated, preferring to live amongst others speaking the same language, wearing similar clothes, and having the same culture and background. The most notable such areas were the Altmaha Valley in

Georgia, the Mohawk and Upper Hudson Valleys in New York and the Cape Fear Valley in North Carolina; also Prince Edward Island and Pictou in Nova Scotia. On the outbreak of the American War of Independence, the great majority of those in the Cape Fear region of North Carolina remained firm Loyalists and in 1777 left for Canada, as did those in New York.

The Highlanders also seem to have retained their native dress and habit of bearing arms when they emigrated, despite the stern laws in the Highlands against the latter after 1715 and against both after 1745. In 1736 Governor Oglethorpe of Georgia, visiting some Highlanders on the frontier which they were defending against both Spaniards and Indians, found them wearing the kilt and plaid and armed with broadswords, muskets, and targes, which he described as 'small round shields'. He himself tactfully wore full Highland garb when with them.

In 1737, in Saratoga, Highland dress 'was then a Novelty in the Country', but the Indians were delighted with it. In North Carolina, although of several different clans, the settlers wore their distinctive tartans, kilts, and plaids. As late as 1775 Scots in full Highland dress and equipped with broadswords, muskets, targes, and dags, or pistols, were still arriving at American ports, which would seem to indicate that the Disarming Acts were not being strictly enforced.

In 1739, when war with Spain appeared imminent, the Independent Companies in the Highlands were incorporated into a Regiment of Foot. It consisted of ten companies made up of 850 men wearing the Black Watch tartan and was commanded by the Earl of Crawford. It was to be the forerunner of eighty-six other Highland regiments raised between then and 1815, not including numerous Overseas Highland Regiments.

In 1734 the Black Watch, or 42nd Royal Highland Regiment, as they were to become known, were posted to Flanders to take part in the War of the Austrian Succession. Their Colonel, Lt Colonel Sir Robert Munro of Foulis, obtained permission for them to fight in their own way and at Fontenoy in 1745 they excelled. It was recorded:

According to the usage of his countrymen he ordered the regiment to clap to the ground on receiving the French fire. Instantly after its discharge the men sprang up and coming close to the enemy poured their shot upon them to the certain destruction of multitudes and drove them precipitately back through their own lines; then retreating, drew up again and attacked a second time in the same manner. These attacks they repeated several times in the same day to the surprise of the whole army.

In the same year Prince Charles Edward Stuart, the Young Pretender, son of James VII and II, made his last desperate bid for power. It should be noted that at best his army consisted of only 5,000 men, some of whom were Lowlanders. From amongst some 300,000 Highlanders, he only succeeded in raising support from the largely Roman Catholic and Episcopalian Camerons, Stewarts, and Macdonalds, who were in any event opposed to the Whig and Presbyterian Campbells, the principal Government supporters.

The entire mismanaged, mad, desperate, and gallant affair ended predictably in disaster at Culloden. Yet it had so very nearly succeeded, against all the odds. When Prince Charles reached Derby, only 130 miles from London, George II was making plans for flight to the Continent. If the father had made as bold an attempt a mere thirty years earlier, he might well have carried all before him. In the meantime the climate of opinion had altered. The son was just too late and Culloden sounded the knell of his hopes and the end of the clan system. It would be wrong, however, to think of Culloden as the cause of this, for the clans were already doomed and failing and there was more than a hint of desperation, of a last fling, in the rebellion of 1745.

The old Highland way of life had already gone for ever, although many had not fully realized it. The end had come with the building of Wade's roads. It was no longer reasonable to expect Lowlanders to pay 'Blackmeal', or protection money, to prevent their cattle being rustled. There was no longer room for a semi-martial feudal system within the modern state. Willy-nilly, the clansmen had to abide by the laws of the land. Thus Culloden may be seen as one part of Scotland, half Highland and half Lowland, settling this issue with another part, all Highland. The aftermath was grim simply because of the totally callous behaviour of the Hanoverian Duke of Cumberland, giving no quarter even to the wounded and harrying with fire and sword.

Following the 1745 rebellion, scarcely surprisingly, the Disarming Acts were more rigorously and intensively enforced, and further repressive Acts were passed. The wearing of the kilt or tartan was forbidden, along with the carrying or possession of arms. It was, of course, forbidden to remit rent in return for armed service to the chief. The Acts did change the Highland way of life, but as has already been emphasized it was changing in any event, and they merely speeded up the process. They certainly resulted in a steady flow of emigrants southwards on the new roads, many of whom went overseas. They also ensured a steady flow of recruits to the Highland regiments, where it was possible both to wear the kilt and bear arms.

Once again, despite strongly held notions to the contrary, there was no immediate transportation of large numbers of Jacobite prisoners. Again, only some 800 appear to have been sent abroad to the plantations as bond-servants. It is true that the Acts decreed that anyone caught with arms was, on the first occasion, liable to be sent to America as a soldier and on the second to transportation for seven years. Those guilty of wearing Highland dress on a second conviction were also to be transported for seven years.

These laws may account for some enforced emigrants, but just how harshly, or otherwise, the laws were enforced must have largely depended on the individuals enforcing them. General Stuart of Garth, an acknowledged authority on the Highlanders in the early nineteenth century, wrote that many Highlanders ignored the Disarming Acts, adding: 'An old gentleman of Athole, a friend of mine, Mr Robertson of Auchleeke, carried this spirit so far, that disobeying all restrictions against carrying arms, he never laid them aside, and even wore his dirk when sitting in his dining room, until his death in his 87th year.' Since General Stuart was writing in 1822, it seems likely that the gentleman referred to carried out his open disobedience in the 1770s and early 80s, when the Acts had generally fallen into disuse. The probability is that after the first decade little real notice was taken of these Acts, except in cases of blatant contravention.

Since the Highlanders emigrating seemed able to bring out arms with them as a matter of course, it would seem that the Disarming Acts did not forbid the making of swords and pistols, but merely wearing them. Presumably anyone leaving the country was able to buy arms quite openly, aware that he would not subsequently be contravening the law by carrying them in the Highlands.

Certainly the famous dag-makers of Doune in Perthshire, manufacturers of long barrelled pistols of beautiful balance, with butts terminating in a characteristic ramshorn, or double scroll, were not hampered by the Acts. Such craftsmen as John Campbell, Christie and four generations of Caddells, who all came from this small area, were famed throughout Scotland. As well as being excellently balanced and wonderfully proportioned, their pistols were richly decorated and engraved with silver or gold, making them works of art in any century. On some of the finer examples, the delicate scroll-work and inlaid tracery appears almost like silver lace encasing the pistol. The merging of butt and barrel is a masterpiece of line and perfection of balance.

From around 1700 to 1790, throughout the whole period when the Disarming Acts were most effective in the Highlands, these pistols were being steadily produced from this small Highland village. As examples of Scottish craftsmanship and, on a higher plane, as an example of art, they stand alongside anything of a similar kind anywhere. It is significant that, with the end of the eighteenth century, there is a steady decline in their style and craftsmanship, mirroring the general decline of craftsmanship in Scotland caused largely by the emigration of skilled workers seeking better rewards in the south or overseas.

By the middle of the century, Scots were spreading throughout the Empire, both from the Highlands and Lowlands. A typical example is that of the sons of Sir Robert Dalrymple of North Berwick – five sons and three daughters by his first wife and at least four sons by his second wife. His fourth son by his second marriage was sent out to India in the service of the East India Company in 1753, dying in Bengal in 1756 at the start of a promising career. His brothers had a variety of professions and occupations, including soldier, doctor, Member of Parliament and merchant in Cadiz, which indicates the widespread interests of only one family. Multiplied countless times over, it may be appreciated how very widely the Scots were spreading throughout the Empire and the world, and also the power and influence they came to wield.

On the continent of Europe there were still Scots who, from

choice or necessity, were making a career as mercenaries rather than as merchants or in more peaceful spheres. The Keith brothers, George and James, the former tenth Earl Marishal, both attainted after the rebellion of 1715, were good examples. Both initially served as officers in the Spanish army, but from 1728 to 1747 James served under Tsar Peter II of Russia, attaining the rank of General. He then offered his services to Frederick II of Prussia, who promoted him to the rank of Field Marshal. Frederick II also employed his brother George in several diplomatic posts, having a high regard for both of them. Receiving a royal pardon from George II, George returned to Scotland, but James was killed at the battle of Hochkirchen in 1758 and buried with full military honours.

In Canada the threat of an imminent war with France in 1755 caused Charles Lawrence, Governor of Nova Scotia, to expel the peaceful French Acadian settlers on the incorrect assumption that in such an event they might prove a threat; not appreciating that in fact they wished no part of any European conflict. In their place he invited American settlers to take up land. Alexander MacNutt, a well-named Ulster adventurer, persuaded some 600 Ulster Scots, who had formed the settlement of Londonderry in New Hampshire amongst others, to move there and form the new settlements of Truro, Londonderry, and Onslow.

Notably anti-English, these 'Scotch-Irish' as they were often termed, were amongst many Ulster Scots who had settled in America from 1720 onwards. Never easy with their neighbours, troublesome, idle, and quarrelsome, they were easily confused with the Scots in the minds of those who did not appreciate that they were Scots at one remove. In their new settlements they reverted to the old pre-emigrant Lowland ways, growing flax and weaving linen from it.

In 1756, the Seven Years War between France and England began and more Highland regiments were promptly recruited. Major General David Stuart of Garth, writing in his book *Sketches of the Character, Manners and Present State of the Highlanders of Scotland, with Details of the Military Service of the Highland Regiments* noted:

In the year 1755, when the establishment of the regiment (The 42nd Royal Highland Regiment, or Black Watch) was augmented preparatory to the war, the Laird of Mackintosh, then a Captain in the regiment, had charge of all the recruiting parties . . . to the Highlands, and quickly collected 500 men, the number he was desired to recruit. Of these he enlisted 87 men in one forenoon.

One morning as he was sitting at breakfast in Inverness, 38 men of the name Macpherson, from Badenoch, appeared in front of the window, with the offer of their services to Mackintosh; their own immediate chief, the Laird of Cluny, being then in exile, in consequence of his attainder after the Rising. The late General Skinner of the engineers was at breakfast with Mackintosh that morning; and being newly arrived in that part of the country, the whole scene, with all its circumstances, made an impression on his mind which he never forgot.

Stuart went on to note that when the Highland regiments landed in America their appearance attracted much notice. 'The Indians in particular were delighted to see a European regiment so similar to their own.' He quoted a New Yorker who wrote:

When the Highlanders landed they were caressed by all ranks and orders of men, but more particularly by the Indians. On the march to Albany, the Indians flocked from all quarters to see the strangers, who, they believed, were of the same extraction as themselves, and therefore received them as brothers.

Among the Highland regiments raised for the war in America were Montgomerie's Highlanders, or the 77th, formed in 1757. They also served in Martinique and Havana. At the end of the war in 1763, they were offered land in America, those who accepted mostly settling in the Cape Fear region of North Carolina. Fraser's Highlanders, or the 78th and 71st regiments, were also raised at the same time. They fought at Louisburg and Quebec with Wolfe and were also offered land in America when the war was over.

It should be appreciated that some emigrants went neither of their own free will and volition, nor transported by due process of law. In 1757 a small book was published entitled *The Life and Curious Adventures of Peter Williamson, who was carried off from Aberdeen and sold for a slave.* In this, Peter Williamson of Aberdeenshire recounted how he was kidnapped as a child of ten in 1740, along with several other children, at the instigation of certain Aberdeen magistrates. He was shipped to Philadelphia and there sold as a bond-servant for £16. His master proved to be a kindly time-expired Scottish bond-servant who had prospered and by then owned his own plantation. He taught Peter Williamson to read and write, and on his death, soon after Peter Williamson came of age, left him his estate in his will.

Peter Williamson was subsequently captured by Indians and forced to act as a slave to them. He finally escaped and at last returned to Aberdeen. There he exhibited himself in Indian dress and became known as 'Indian Peter'. Sued by the magistrates for libel on the publication of his book, he countersued and obtained substantial damages. It is apparent from his book that from the 1660s onwards there had been a regular trade in people thus kidnapped and sold as bond-servants to the plantations. It seems that unscrupulous magistrates and shipowners were not averse to making a profit by such means and the trade can hardly have been restricted to Aberdeen.

By the mid-eighteenth century, of course, the time had long passed when, as at the end of the seventeenth century, the town council of Stirling needed to note the purchase of two fathoms of rope 'to tye Laurence McLairen quhen sent to America'. There might still be some reluctance to going out as a bond-servant, but there was certainly little objection to going to America. Some convicted rebels might have been sent out as bond-servants after the 1745 rebellion and others might have been sentenced for offences such as carrying arms, but many others again might have gone voluntarily. How many were victims of treatment similar to Peter Williamson's it is simply impossible to say.

In 1759, Wolfe led the Highlanders in a surprise attack on Quebec, where on the Fields of Abraham (named after Abraham Martin '*dit L'Ecossais*') the French were defeated and the city was captured for the second time. James Murray, the commander who took over on Wolfe's death, found himself with a total lack of supplies, even of blankets, and in the first severe winter with sub-zero temperatures the Scots suffered greatly. The French appear to have been amazingly sympathetic in the circumstances, the nuns even knitting long stockings for the Highlander's legs, to go under their kilts and prevent frostbite. As ever, the French and the Scots seem to have got on well together. Although there were numerous casualties, many of Fraser's Highlanders and the Black Watch elected to settle in Canada when the war was over.

In the meantime, various industrial enterprises were starting in Scotland. In the Highlands, lead-mining was attempted without much success and iron-smelting was also tried, rather more successfully, using local timber. In the Lowlands, one of the outstanding ventures was the formation of the Carron Iron Works which was started by two Englishmen, John Roebuck and Samuel Garbett, in conjunction with a Scot, William Cadell, at Falkirk. This was one of the first fruits of the Union in the field of economic and industrial co-operation in Scotland.

The diversity of the Carron Iron Works products was from the first remarkable, ranging from pots, pans, anvils, ploughs, shovels, pails, stoves and grates to cannonballs and cannon. The carronade, a naval close-action cannon, was specifically one of its products, taking its name from the Works and being used extensively on shipboard throughout the wars with France up to 1815. The Carron Iron Works was also fortunate in having the services of the Adam brothers as designers, producing intricate and graceful designs for fireplaces.

In 1760, when the British army, bolstered by the newly formed Highland regiments in conjunction with other Scottish regiments, had become successful as seldom before, George II died. His grandson, the twenty-two-year old George III, succeeded him, still very much influenced by 'his dear friend' and erstwhile tutor, the Earl of Bute, First Lord of the Treasury and, as was well known inside and outside Court circles, his mother's lover. At least George III, later to be known as bluff 'Farmer George', was the first Hanoverian able to speak intelligible English.

In 1762 Admiral Sir George Lockhart, a Lowlander of the family of Lockhart of Lee, by taking the family name Ross inherited the estate of Balnagowan in Ross-shire. Retired from the sea, he brought his energies to bear on his newly acquired estate and started by introducing sheep, which to everyone's surprise proved extremely profitable. His neighbours soon began to follow his example. It was a short step from that to clearing away the impoverished 'townships' of miserable sod huts and uneconomic holdings worked on the old 'runrig' system (cultivating intermixed strips in open fields, as in feudal times) and replacing them with highy profitable flocks of sheep. The infamous Clearances had begun.

In the same calamitous year the Earl of Bute was made Prime Minister. The first Scot to hold the post, it was unfortunate that he was in no way fitted for it. With his background, and the fact that he was now widely known to be the Dowager Princess's lover, there was nothing he could conceivably have done which would have been regarded by the English mob as anything but bad. Even the Peace of Paris, which he negotiated in 1763 to end the Seven Years War, was hailed as 'a shameful peace'. During his period in office the many Scots in England were subjected to a campaign of vilification which has never been exceeded. Graffiti on the walls, editorials in the newspapers, pamphlets, and riotous mobs were all, unanimously and emphatically, anti-Scots. The effect was such that numbers of Scots living in England felt it necessary to change, or at least modify, their names. Thus a Mackay might drop the 'Mac' and become, less conspicuously Kay, possibly adding an 'e' to produce the old English name of Kaye.

Bute was by no means the only Scot in an influential position at Court. Allan Ramsay was the Court painter and the Adam brothers were the Court architects. Many other Scots were merchants and bankers in the City, in Government posts, in the army or the navy. When Bute used his influence to place mediocre Scots in positions of authority, this was naturally resented, especially since he made little effort to conceal such actions.

Understandably the English masses, their fears of the Scots during the 1745 rebellion still not forgotten, bitterly resented the influx. Since many Scots took posts as excise officials, this merely intensified feelings of dislike. Resentment against them was focused on the person of Bute by John Wilkes in his scurrilous news-sheet *The North Briton*. During the Wilkes riots of 1763, when boots and petticoats were burnt at street corners (satirizing Bute and his liaison with the Dowager Princess) the anti-Scots fervour was probably at its height, but such feelings once roused are not easily forgotten. As late as 1773 Johnson had to be assured by Boswell that it was quite unnecessary for him to arm himself with pistols before setting off on their famous tour of the Highlands.

By this time certain effects of the Union were becoming obvious in Scotland as more and more Scots, whether from the

Highlands or Lowlands, were moving south, or at any rate out of Scotland. On the Firth of Forth the once flourishing mercantile ports were falling into gradual decay with the ending of the Continental trade and the exodus of the rich merchants to the south. Further north the military roads had opened up the Highlands with a vengeance, and, as we have seen, many Highlanders were taking advantage of them to emigrate, either to North America or to England, even if only for seasonal work on the harvest.

In the Lowlands, a steady improvement in agriculture following the adoption of new ideas from the south was now the noticeable feature, with enclosures being built apace and new root crops, crop rotations, and methods of farming being tried and accepted. Different systems of land tenure were also being introduced with considerable success, for as long as the tenant had no security of tenure he was unlikely to try to improve his land. Inevitably to some extent these experiments resulted in a measure of depopulation, but new industry and invention were flourishing with the aid of capital from the south, as witness the Carron Iron Works at Falkirk, soon followed by similar industrial innovations. The most significant advance of all, however, came in 1764, when James Watt invented the steam engine which was to revolutionize life in both Scotland and England, and indeed in the world, over the ensuing hundred years or more.

Throughout the Highlands new methods of agriculture were slower to be adopted than in the Lowlands, but the introduction of the potato provided a staple diet in times of famine. The ease of supplying relief via the military roads also meant that, even then, few died. The introduction of vaccination against smallpox also had a very considerable effect in checking deaths, especially amongst children. So, not surprisingly, the population of the Highlands increased despite the steady drain of emigration and military service.

The position of the chieftain was now being steadily eroded, changing merely to that of landlord. Whereas it had always been a matter of pride for him to surround himself with a lengthy 'tail' of followers and dependants, he was no longer allowed to keep a private army. His tacksmen, once the important buttress between chieftain and clansmen, who ensured that when called to arms his followers would respond, were now merely middlemen, living by

'The last of the clan', by I. C. Brown RSA, engraved by W. Richardson –
another heart-rending Victorian picture.

leasing the land at a low rent from the chieftain and collecting a
higher rent from their tenants. The obvious first step, when a
chieftain was short of funds, was to increase the tacksmen's rent,
and it was precisely this that caused many tacksmen (together
with lesser chieftains and men of substance) to gather considerable numbers of tenants together, sell up their belongings and
emigrate to North America.

Between 1768 and 1772 about 3,000 Highlanders were estimated to have emigrated to the Cape Fear districts of North
Carolina. (Ironically considerable numbers seem to have settled
in Cumberland County, called after the Duke whose name was

anathema in the Highlands following Culloden). The climate there was warmer than in Scotland, with longer summers and shorter winters. The soil was easily worked and reasonably fertile. In all it was estimated that by 1775 something like 12,000 Highlanders had probably settled in this area in North Carolina alone.

The 3,000 who emigrated to the Cape Fear district were only a small part of the overall numbers emigrating at this time. It was from 1763 to 1775 that an 'epidemical fury of emigration' affected the Highlands. The estimated figures for those emigrating to North America during this period are around 24,000. By later standards this was not a very large number, but by the standards of the day it was a considerable loss to Scotland.

During his tour with Dr Johnson, Boswell recorded in 1773, while on Skye:

> We had again a good dinner and in the evening a great dance . . . And then . . . a dance which I suppose the emigration from Skye has occasioned. They call it 'America' . . . It goes on till all are set a-going, setting and wheeling round each other . . . It shows how emigration catches till all are set afloat. Mrs Mackinnon told me that last year when the ship sailed from Portree for America, the people on shore were almost distracted when they saw their relatives go off they lay down on the ground and tumbled and tore the grass with their teeth. This year there was not a tear shed. The people on shore seemed to think that they would soon follow.

The hard winter of 1771, cattle blight, and increased rents, resulted in some 700 Macdonalds leaving Skye for America in 1772 and more following in 1773. In a time of need, letters from settlers already doing well in America were enough to tip the scales in favour of emigration. Once the decision had been made by sufficient numbers, others soon joined them, and it was thus the 'epidemical fury' gripped both Highlanders and Islanders.

An indication of the number of Highlanders in North America as early as 1768 is afforded by the fact that a certain George Bartram, a Scots merchant in Philadelphia, found it worthwhile to advertise for sale: *Best Scotch plaids for gentlemen's gowns and boy's highland dress.* Clearly anyone buying a kilt for his son in North

America at this period was likely to do so only from first-hand knowledge of Scotland, and presumably Bartram's principal sales were to Highlanders who had emigrated, or settled there after serving in the Seven Years War.

In the early 1770s a great many Lowlanders emigrated to North America after the failure of the Douglas, Heron and Company's 'Ayr Bank'. Formed in 1769 without a single banker amongst its 136 stockholders, this rash venture issued bills to the value of £400,000 against a capital of £150,000. By various expedients it survived until the inevitable crash, in 1773. Meanwhile there had been other bankruptcies owing to similar rash issuing of bills against non-existent capital.

Thousands of weavers, particularly, and similar artisans in the towns were unable to obtain work and were forced to emigrate by indenting themselves for service in America. On Lowland farms the inflation resulting from the crash meant an increase in rents, and a consequent emigration from the countryside as well. Small farmers tended to join together and form associations for the purpose of emigrating as a group.

A good example of the latter was the Scots-American Company of Farmers, also known as the 'Inchinnan Company' as most of the members came from that part of Renfrew. Formed in 1773, it was composed of 139 members. Their agents, David Allen and James Whitelaw (later the Surveyor General of Vermont) were sent to find land in America and encountered the Rev. Dr John Witherspoon, then President of the College of New Jersey, Princeton. He offered them land in Ryegate, which they bought, and by 1774 the first settlers had arrived. A similar company which was formed in Stirlingshire, and whose agent was Colonel Alexander Harvey, settled in 1774 in Barnet close to Ryegate and the two settlements ultimately became Caledonia County, Vermont. There were more than 5,000 immigrants in 1774, although this included some Highlanders, and the stream only ceased in 1775 when the Government prohibited further emigration.

Meanwhile the Scots were gathering in India also, in the East India Company's service. George Gray, born in Bengal, the son of an East Lothian doctor serving in India in 1737, was schooled in Scotland, but returned to India in 1755. By 1765 he was on the Governor's Council in Calcutta and was Town Collector. Here by devious means he made a fortune, and found it prudent to retire and return to Scotland in the 1770s. Archibald Swinton, another prominent Scot in India, a doctor whose fortunes were bound up with Clive's, first went out in 1752 and returned finally to Scotland in 1765. His fortune was considerable and amongst the early nabobs he was notable for being able to afford to buy two estates on his return home.

By the 1770s unrest in America was beginning to manifest itself increasingly plainly. In 1773 the famous Boston Tea Party took place, when high-spirited young men dressed as Indians made their views on the taxation methods of the British Government very clear. The fuse had been laid, and the match was struck in 1775 when the Massachusetts militia attacked British forces at Lexington and Concord. Once more, Scots found themselves fighting on two sides overseas.

[4]

From 1775 to 1875, the 'Emigration Century'

At the outbreak of the War of American Independence the Scots were very much disliked in America. In part this was probably a reflection of their unpopularity in England, an aftermath of the unfortunate Bute ministry. In part it may also have been due to the clannishness of the Scots, particularly of the Highlanders settled in the Cape Fear district of North Carolina, in the Mohawk Valley of New York, in New Jersey, and in Pennsylvania, where they tended to form distinct ethnic groups retaining their own language and garb and failing to integrate with other settlers. Another undoubted reason was their very pronounced Loyalist sympathies. Perhaps the decisive reason, however, was simply their ubiquitous presence in all walks of life, but predominantly amongst the professional classes. It was as much as anything else their success which made them disliked, as well as the fact that more and more of them seemed to be arriving every year.

As in England, during the comparatively short time since 1707 when they had been granted equal opportunities for trading in the colonies, the Scots had prospered too well. Within fifty years they had suddenly appeared everywhere in positions of power and influence. They were to be found as officers in the army, even in non-Scottish regiments, in administration from governor downwards, as lawyers, doctors, and bankers, as leaders in religion and education, taking an active part in politics (generally as Tories supporting the government), and above all as merchants.

In Virginia especially, the Scots merchants' stranglehold on the plantation owners, owing to the latter's complete lack of business acumen, caused them to be particularly disliked. In a good many other areas Scots merchants were also disliked for their pronounced Loyalist sympathies, which were natural enough since many of them had close links, if not actual partnerships, with family firms in Scotland. Inevitably they had a vested interest in maintaining the *status quo* of settled government, because to do otherwise was clearly to jeopardize their livelihood.

In Scotland itself more Highland regiments were hastily raised to fight in America with the outbreak of the War of Independence. The 71st or Fraser's Highlanders, raised in 1775, served at Brooklyn, Savannah, and York River, being reduced in 1783. The Argyll Highlanders were raised in 1777, sailing for Halifax, Nova Scotia in 1778 and being stationed there for the entire war. In action at Penobscot they too were reduced in 1783. Macdonald's Highlanders, or the old 76th, were raised between 1777 and 1784 by Lord Macdonald. They fought in Virginia, and on Lord Cornwallis's surrender were taken prisoner. There were no desertions while prisoners and they were reduced in 1784.

Particularly notable was the first Highland regiment to be raised outside Scotland. The Royal Highland Emigrant Regiment, or old 84th Highland Regiment, was recruited in 1775 from Highland emigrants in Canada who had been discharged from the 42nd Black Watch, or Fraser's and Montgomerie's Highlanders, and who had settled in America after the Peace of Paris in 1763. They defended Quebec and a second battalion was formed, both of which were reduced in 1783. Another regiment, composed mostly of Catholic Highlanders from Glen Urquhart, Glenmoriston, and Glengarry, notably the Macdonnells, was recruited by Sir John Johnson in 1776 from his lands in the Mohawk Valley, whence he led them to Quebec.

Although on the face of it most Highlanders might appear to have emigrated to escape a life of poverty and wretchedness, and thus might have been expected to espouse the Republican cause in America, there were other factors involved. Most were only too well aware of events after Culloden, when they had last seen the House of Hanover challenged. Many had also gone out to America at the urging of their tacksmen, whose leadership they were accustomed to follow, and the tacksmen were often erstwhile officers who had served in the army and still retained their loyalty to the Crown. The strong Loyalist sympathies of most Highlanders were well known, especially in the Cape Fear region where the Governor expected to be able to raise some 3,000 loyal troops from amongst them.

In the event, although Governor Martin recommended Allan Macdonald of Kingsburgh (husband of Flora Macdonald) to raise a battalion of 1,000 men, General Gage, the General Officer in Command in that area, had his own ideas and sent a Major Macdonald from Boston in his place. Since Allan Macdonald had been in the colony less than a year, this may well have been a sensible decision. Eventually about 2,000 Highlanders were somewhat reluctantly recruited, and marched under the leadership of a Brigadier Macdonald towards the coast.

At a bridge over Moore's Creek a force of 1,000 Americans under Colonel James Moore awaited the approach of the Highlanders. As they advanced in single file over the partially demolished bridge, the Americans shot some seventy without any difficulty. The rest either fled into the woods or surrendered tamely without fighting. The Americans were left with all the spoils and discarded weapons, as well as about 800 prisoners. As a battle it had been a farce and, not altogether surprisingly in view of the number of Macdonalds involved in the leadership, it later became known mockingly as the 'Insurrection of the Clan Macdonald'. It can only be concluded that the Highlanders' hearts were not really in it, for they could certainly have put up a much better showing. This was not a point, however, that told in their favour and for the rest of the war they were to suffer a certain degree of persecution.

In 1775 a contrasting example was set by a Highlander, Donald McLeod, newly arrived from Scotland, who petitioned the New York Congress for permission to raise a company of a hundred Highlanders from a shipload of immigrants, 'with the Proviso of having Liberty to wear their own Country Dress Commonly called the Highland Habit'. They were 'already furnished with Guns, Swords, Pistols and Highland Dirks which . . . are at this Time very difficult to be had'. While this appears to be among the few records of Highlanders offering to fight for the Republican cause, there does not seem to be any report of them actually seeing service.

There is, however, a record of a Philadelphian writing to a friend in London in 1776: 'Many of the Scots have particularly signalised themselves in the cause of freedom . . . Messrs. Sproat, Semple and Milligan, merchants . . . have raised companies of their own countrymen of a hundred men each, who are equipped in the Scottish dress and make a very warlike appearance. I mention this, as I see many reflections on the Scotch in the

English papers. Thank God, they are here the very earnest advocates of liberty.'

Despite the defection of massive numbers of Highlanders, who might have been expected to support them, there were many Scots prominent in the Republican ranks, though mostly second- and third-generation settlers. A good example among the signatories of the Declaration of Independence was Colonel George Ross, descended from the Rosses of Balblair, a distinguished family of Scots colonists. Another who signed the Declaration of Independence was Philip Livingston, a third-generation American Scot descended from the Rev. John Livingston, Minister of Ancrum in 1663, who was forced to fly to the Continent, to Rotterdam, because of religious persecution. Yet another was Lewis Morris, son of Chief Justice Lewis Morris, a second-generation American Scot, a graduate of Yale in 1746 and a farmer on a large scale. In addition there was Thomas McKean, later Governor of Pennsylvania, whose father had emigrated from Londonderry in 1725.

Exceptional was the case of the Rev. Dr John Witherspoon, another Scottish signatory, who had been born in Gifford, East Lothian, in 1723. The son of the manse, he himself graduated from Edinburgh University in 1739, becoming a minister in 1745. In 1757 he was minister at Paisley, before going to America where in 1768 he became President of the College of New Jersey, later Princeton University. As such he played his part in framing the Declaration of Independence, which may explain certain resemblances it bears to the Scottish Declaration of Arbroath.

In all, eleven members of Congress at the time of the Declaration of Independence were of Scots origin. In addition to this, no less than nine of George Washington's brigadier-generals were Scots, and without one Scot in particular his navy would have been sadly lacking. John Paul Jones, born plain John Paul in Kirkcudbright, son of a gardener, apprenticed to a shipmaster in Whitehaven, was the founder of the American navy. In 1778 he descended on the coast of Scotland and conducted a successful raid against English shipping, defeating superior forces of the British navy in an outstanding two-ship action.

When the War of Independence ended, the bulk of the Highland settlers of recent origin (that is, within a decade or so, when there had been exceptionally high levels of emigration) felt bound to move from the Carolinas and New York to Canada. These Scottish settlers became known as the United Empire Loyalists, and their movements form a saga in themselves. With them, the focus of Scottish emigration after the American Revolution shifted to Canada.

As was the case with the Scots in England during and after the persecution suffered as a result of the Bute regime, emigrant Scots remaining in America adopted a low profile, both during and after the Revolution. The bulk of the Scottish settlements, with groups of Highland emigrants speaking only their own language and wearing the kilt, disappeared after the war. There were still plenty of Scots, but in the main they now adapted readily enough to the American way of life. There were still St Andrew's Societies and similar manifestations of Scottish national feeling, but not at first to the same extent as before. Hence today the kilt is not as common in the United States of America as it is in Canada.

With the mass movement of Scots to Canada, the problem arose of where to settle these Loyalists who had trekked out of America and were now homeless. Whether they had fought in the emigrant regiments or in some of the irregular forces raised at that time, or whether they had merely been forced out by persecution, the end result was the same: they were now in Canada and needed somewhere to live.

A small group went to the Niagara peninsula, and others to the Cape Peninsula, while even more found suitable land between Quebec and Vermont. The bulk, however were settled on the upper St Lawrence river near Lake Ontario between Johnstown and Cataraqui, now Kingston. By 1784 nearly 6,000 United Empire Loyalists were pioneering and opening up the ground as far as Cataraqui, 100 miles upriver from the main settlement at New Johnston, now Cornwall.

They were tough and self-sufficient, and by now they knew how to set about taming a wilderness. They cut down trees for log cabins, cleared ground for crops, made clothes and shoes from skins, tapped maple trees for sugar, and produced their own corn whisky. Even so, they suffered famine after an exceptionally bad winter in 1787 and had to apply to the government for relief. Furthermore, they wished to be ruled by British rather than French law, and they also petitioned on this score. The end result was that in 1789 the region of Upper Canada was formed.

A further migration after the American War of Independence resulted in some 30,000 Scottish Loyalists moving from New York, New Jersey, Carolina, Maine, and Pennsylvania by sea to Halifax, Nova Scotia. Here they settled on forfeited land held by absentee holders who had never taken up their grants. Those from Carolina found the climate particularly fierce after the softer winters to which they had become accustomed there. In 1784 the north of the Bay of Fundy was named as a new colonial province, New Brunswick. A further post-war settlement was opened up at Pictou on the northern shore of Nova Scotia. The Scots who settled here were joined in 1786 by a Presbyterian minister named James Macgregor, who learned Gaelic in order to preach to the widest possible congregation.

With the end of the war came a fresh spate of emigration from Scotland. The harsh Scottish winter of 1783 saw famine barely staved off in the Highlands through the distribution of relief made possible by the military roads. This was a factor which convinced many Highlanders that the only course open to them was emigration. Letters and messages from soldiers serving in North America, or relations who had emigrated previously, describing the wonderful opportunities in Canada, also acted as a powerful encouragement to emigration.

The familiar complaints – rising rents, uncertainty of tenure, poverty – and the desire to join relations already abroad, were the principal reasons ascribed for wishing to emigrate. Evictions rarely seem to have been mentioned as a reason for wishing to leave the country. Increasingly, indeed, landlords were doing their best to prevent too much emigration on the grounds that the country needed the people. It was inevitably those skilled craftsmen and men of ability who could least be spared who were choosing to emigrate.

It was now no longer the tacksmen who were leading large parties abroad, but more often their ministers and priests. Increasingly, also, shiploads were organized by agents acting as entrepreneurs, encouraging people to emigrate with broadsheets which often presented totally false pictures of what they might expect. Conditions on some of the emigrant ships at this period were grim in the extreme, with inadequate provisions and sanitary facilities, so that disease often took its toll.

By this time the old colonial system of serving a period of

indenture as a bond-servant had completely lapsed. Settlers were now faced with the often daunting prospect of clearing virgin land and surviving as best as they could. Many cases arose, of course, where the prospective settlers were destitute on arrival and had to be helped with food, clothing, and money to set them on their feet. Frequently such shiploads proved a considerable burden on the port where they landed, which very often proved to be Pictou. After a period of recuperation and adjustment, such settlers very often moved on to other areas, either where they already had friends or relations, or where they felt they could do better.

In Scotland from 1780 onwards more Highland regiments were raised for service in India. Amongst these were the famous 2nd Battalion of the 42nd, or Royal Highland Regiment, the Black Watch, which was raised in 1780 and became the 73rd after the siege of Mangalore. The 74th Highland Regiment of Foot was raised in 1787, and embarked for India the following year, fighting at the battle of Assaye and finally returning to Britain in 1805. The 75th Regiment, or First Battalion Gordon Highlanders, was also raised in 1787 for service in India and returned in 1806.

On the outbreak of war with the newly declared Republic of France in 1793, further Highland regiments were raised. Alan Cameron of Erracht raised the Queen's Own Cameron Highlanders, and Francis Mackenzie, afterwards Lord Seaforth, raised the 78th Highlanders, or 2nd Battalion Seaforth Highlanders. Another battalion of the Seaforth Highlanders was raised in 1794. In the same year, 1794, the Duke of Argyll raised the 91st Princess Louise's Argyllshire Highlanders, and the Marquis of Huntly raised the 92nd, later the 2nd Battalion Gordon Highlanders. Finally the 93rd, or Sutherland Highlanders were raised in 1800 and in 1813 a second battalion was also raised and sent to Newfoundland.

By 1795 the second spate of emigration, following the War of Independence, had virtually ceased, for once war with France was declared there was little opportunity. The uncertainty of sea-voyages, and the need to recruit men for the army and navy, were such that emigration, except during the period around the Peace of Amiens in 1802, was not easily accomplished. The fact, too, that for a short time, from 1812 to 1814, the United States of America was also at war with Britain further inhibited attempts at emigration. Only after 1815 did the steady flow begin once more. Nevertheless Scots continued to go to India, America, and the West Indies, both on business and as emigrants, although such traffic was necessarily considerably reduced.

During the Peace of Amiens and the brief lull in the Napoleonic Wars, there was a sudden spate of emigration to Canada. In 1802, 800 Roman Catholics from Barra settled in Antigonish with their priests, Alexander and Augustin Macdonald. In 1803, Thomas Douglas, eighth Earl of Selkirk, who believed emigration was the cure for the Highlander's problems, led 800 emigrants from Skye, Ross, Inverness and Argyll to Prince Edward Island, where they formed a successful settlement inspired by his active leadership (see p. 114).

One involuntary source of emigration remained during this period. From 1787 onwards convict ships were sailing regularly to Botany Bay in Australia. Between 1788 and 1820 nearly 26,000 convicts, of whom some 3,500 were female, were transported to New South Wales and Tasmania, or Van Diemen's Land as it was then known. How many Scots were amongst these involuntary settlers it is impossible to say, but there were certainly a number of Scots amongst the administrators.

The outbreak of war against France meant more to Scotland than merely recruiting soldiers for overseas service, whether Highland or Lowland. The recruitment of Fencible regiments as a form of Home Defence force also went on apace and a considerable number were raised during the years 1793 to 1802, when most of them were reduced. The shipyards along the coast, especially in Aberdeen, were busy producing wooden-hulled ships for the navy and the merchant fleet. Ironworks such as the Carron works at Falkirk were soon busy turning out war supplies (in their case, particularly carronades for the navy) as fast as they could produce them. The kelp industry in the Highlands, producing alkali, flourished, since it was in short supply and much in demand for chemical processes, such as making soap and dyes. In the Lowlands there was more intensive agriculture, as inevitably the price of food rose.

The period saw a literary renaissance, with Robert Burns, Allan Ramsay, James Hogg (the Ettrick Shepherd), and, of course, Sir Walter Scott. Although Robert Burns's future international reputation was to be as the poet of the people, it was Sir

Walter Scott, the Establishment figure, who cast his 'Wizard's Mantle' of romance over Scotland, obscuring the harsh images of her history and the equally harsh truths of much that was happening in the Highlands. The agricultural revolution had already taken place and now the industrial revolution was under way. In 1812 the first steamboat ever launched puffed its way down the Clyde, a precursor of what was to come on Clydeside.

In India, much that happened during the latter decades of the century was also symbolic of what was to come. The British Raj was in the making and Scots, as usual, were to the fore in the process. By this time many were in positions of considerable power and influence, returning home to build themselves large family seats in true nabob style. Outstanding perhaps was Allan Macpherson, who served from 1764 to 1784 as soldier and administrator, returning to build a house at Blairgowrie. In much the same period, 1772 to 1784, another notable administrator was Robert Lindsay, who returned to build a house at Balcarres in Fife.

Among various family combinations, the Murray Macgregor brothers, John, Alexander, Peter, and Robert, all served in India from 1770 to 1785, but only Alexander succeeded in making his fortune, and he died on the boat coming home. Another family of brothers, the Grahams, John, Thomas, Robert, and George, served from 1770 to 1800, making their fortunes and building Kinross House on their return. Two other notable nabobs of this period were Captain Thomas Graham of Airth, who served from 1789 to 1796 and returned to build a mansion at Airth in Stirlingshire, and James Balfour, who served from 1796 to 1802. He made a dishonest fortune by victualling the troops and consistently supplying short measure, returning to build a Palladian mansion at Whittingehame in East Lothian. In true nabob style, he directed his architect simply to build it larger than his elder brother's family pile at Balbirnie in Fife.

Perhaps the most outstanding achievement was that of Hugh Cleghorn, Professor of History at St Andrew's University, who was instrumental in the annexation of Ceylon in 1795. He was friendly with the Count de Meuron in Switzerland, who owned the Swiss mercenary regiment which garrisoned Ceylon for the Dutch. De Meuron's brother was in charge of the regiment, which was the mainstay of the Dutch defences. With the backing of Dundas in Scotland, Professor Cleghorn was sent out with his friend the Count to persuade the regiment to change sides and fight for the British. After a hazardous journey lasting eight months the Professor accomplished his strange diplomatic mission and Ceylon was finally surrendered bloodlessly. On the proceeds Cleghorn bought a house near St Andrews.

During the latter half of the eighteenth and early nineteenth centuries many Scots were also prominent in Russia in various spheres, not least in mercantile circles. Under Tsar Peter the Great (whose maternal grandmother was a daughter of the Hamilton family married to a Russian) Major-General James Bruce was Director of the Schools of Navigation, Artillery and Military Engineering. His family, which was a large one, became not only wealthy but extremely influential.

Under Catherine the Great, whose Court banker was named Sutherland, Dr John Rogerson, a Scot from Dumfries, was Imperial physician, a post frequently filled by Scots and one of considerable power. The last Scottish holder of the office was Dr Alexander Crichton, who became physician to Tsar Alexander I in 1804. He was later appointed head of the entire Civil Medical Department at St Petersburg and held this position of great prestige until 1819, when he returned home, soon afterwards to be knighted by George IV.

It was, however, perhaps in naval circles that Scots wielded most influence in Russia during this period. Particularly notable was Admiral Sir Samuel Greig, who joined the Russian Navy in 1763 as a Master's Mate in the Royal Navy. In 1769 Greig (by then a Commander under Rear-Admiral John Elphinston, a fellow Scot who had transferred to the Russian Navy as a Captain RN) helped to destroy the Turkish fleet using fireships under the command of two further Scots Lieutenants named Dugdale and Mackenzie. When Elphinston returned to the Royal Navy, Greig went on to reform the Russian Navy, introducing many Scottish officers, and becoming known as 'Father of the Russian Navy' with the rank of Grand Admiral. He was killed on active service in 1788; but his son Alex Samuilovich became an admiral in the Russian Navy, and a grandson distinguished himself in the Russian forces at the siege of Sebastopol in the Crimean War.

With the end of the war in Europe in 1815, Scotland once more started to send emigrants round the world. The twin problems of overpopulation and lack of employment, especially in the post-war recession, were the irresistible forces behind this surge of emigration. These problems were bad enough in the Lowlands, filled with demobilized soldiers unable to find work, but in the Western Isles they were aggravated by the failure of the kelp industry, which had at least served during the war to provide a living for the Islanders. Unfortunately the alkali produced from the kelp was only in demand as long as the war cut off supplies from Europe.

In 1822 the Australia Company of Edinburgh was founded, the year after Lachlan Macquarie's retirement as Governor of Australia. From this stage onwards there was to be a steady flow of emigrants from Scotland to Australia. In the same year, 1822, Scotland was electrified by the first visit of a reigning monarch since Charles II, which in itself is an indication of the limbo into which the nation had allowed itself to sink since the Union of 1707. George IV, corpulent and corseted, dressed (by the combined efforts of General Sir David Stuart of Garth and Sir Walter Scott) as a Highland Chieftain in the Royal Stuart tartan, with pink silk tights beneath his kilt to preserve the decencies, held Court in Holyrood Palace in Edinburgh. 'In view of the shortness of his stay,' remarked one Edinburgh matron acidly, 'it was thoughtful of His Majesty to show so much of himself to his loyal subjects.'

At this time the Exchequer was losing vast sums annually in Scotland on illicitly distilled whisky, for the duty had been raised progressively and was by then so high that in the Highlands it had become impossible to make a profit by legal methods. The King was given 'the real Glenlivet' whisky to drink when he came to Edinburgh, although it was well known that it had been illicitly distilled. At this period, in the Glenlivet area alone there were said to be over 200 illicit stills. Every Highland farmer who could do so distilled whisky illicitly, simply to pay his rent.

In 1824, however, a new Act was introduced to deal with this absurd situation. By reducing the tax levied on each still, it once again made legal distilling a potentially profitable, as well as a respectable, occupation. As a result, whisky distilling, which had been a backyard craft, slowly developed into a profitable industry. During the nineteenth century it was gradually to become one of the most important industries in Scotland.

In 1825 James Watt's experiments with steam at last bore dramatic fruit with George Stephenson's invention of the railway engine and the opening of the Stockton to Darlington railway. The industrial revolution was in full swing. In Scotland, the population increase was as notable as anywhere else in Britain and it even increased in the Highlands, despite the steady rate of emigration. Sadly, however, there was less and less future for the Highlanders in the Highlands, as increasingly the landlords turned to sheep. The more enlightened and liberal-minded thinkers – whether Highland landlords such as Sir John Sinclair of Ulbster in Caithness, at first advocating the gradual introduction of sheep, or Lowland aristocrats such as the Earl of Selkirk, forming his own settlements of emigrants in Canada, or wealthy industrialists such as David Owen, providing work in special mills – were still unable to provide a real solution to the problem.

The 1820s and 1830s were years of considerable poverty and distress in many parts of Scotland, but the year 1826–7 was particularly grim. It became known as 'the year of the short corn'. Autumn drought affected the crops and semi-starvation aggravated the commercial depression in many districts. The Scottish economy, never very robust, suffered more than it had in many years.

In 1829 a small booklet likely to encourage emigration to America was published, entitled *The Emigrant's Guide in Ten Letters* by William Cobbett, the noted pamphleteer and politician. Having regard to his facility with the pen, it is highly possible that he wrote the entire series of letters himself with a view to their publication at a time when interest in emigration was high. From their style it is certain that he must at least have edited them heavily. If the former was the case, the facts were probably somewhat out of date, because it was ten years since he had been in America. As with so much of Cobbett's work, opinion then was probably as deeply divided as it is now about its authenticity and reliability.

He claimed the *Guide* was composed of 'Several authentic and most interesting Letters from English Emigrants now in America to their Relations in England'. Since they were addressed to a Mr Stephen Watson, Sedlecombe, County of Sussex, England, it is quite possible this *was* a second-generation Scot writing from

America to his father who had emigrated from Scotland to Sussex.

Dearborn County, Indiana, November 29th, 1828.
Dear Father and Mother, We gladly embrace this opportunity of writing to you . . . and we are glad to hear that some of you intend coming to America . . . Here you can rent land by giving one third of what is raised on the land; and a man can get 18 pounds of pork or beef for a day's work, or 3 packs of wheat and every other kind of provision cheap accordingly . . . We advise you to come to New York and up the river Albany where Stephen lives. There you can get information of the road to my house . . . tell James Bridges to come to America if he can for we know that he can get a comfortable living with half the labour he has to do at home. Plenty of land can be bought within twenty miles of our house for one dollar and a quarter an acre. We advise you to come in an American ship . . . John and Mary Watson.

In 1830 William IV came to the throne and the railways began to develop, following the opening of the Manchester to Liverpool railway. In the same year New Zealand was settled. Two years later slavery was abolished throughout the British Empire, an event which was indirectly to have immense repercussions in the United States of America. In 1837 the young Queen Victoria succeeded William IV and a long period of expansion lay ahead.

The 1830s and '40s, however, saw conditions throughout Scotland, especially in the Highlands, take a considerable turn for the worse. There was a tremendous increase in emigration both from Highlands and Lowlands. The introduction of the steam loom meant unemployment and distress for thousands of skilled handloom weavers in the Lowlands. During this period the proportion of skilled craftsmen emigrating from Scotland was very high, with a proportionate fall in the standards of living as a result.

The decline of craftsmanship was emphasized by the Act of 1836 requiring Birmingham hallmarks on any silverwork. Hitherto each Scottish town of any importance had boasted its own silversmiths with its own distinctive hallmarks. There had, admittedly, already been a steady decline in individual Scottish craftsmanship, but from this time forward, for the rest of the century and beyond, little of original worth was produced in this particular field. Nor were the silversmiths the only craftsmen affected by this steady decline in standards, for the majority of craftsmen had either emigrated or moved into one form of industry or another.

In 1843 the issue of patronage in the Scottish church resulted in the formation of the Free Kirk, which seceded from the Church of Scotland in the upheaval known as the Disruption. Like so many religious schisms in Scotland, this had far-reaching results, splitting the Church of Scotland not only in Scotland but also abroad, in Canada and in the Antipodes. Since the Free Kirk was missionary-minded, this may well have helped in the long run to spread the Presbyterian faith abroad.

The royal recognition of Scotland, which started with George IV's visit in 1822 and culminated in the acquisition of Balmoral as a Highland retreat by Queen Victoria and Prince Albert in 1843, had surprisingly important effects. The rediscovery of clan tartans between 1822 and 1850 combined with a growing interest in Highland scenery and an appreciation of the sporting possibilities of hill and loch to change the pattern of life in the Highlands. Where men and cattle had given way to sheep, now in turn sheep gave way to deer and grouse. More and more Englishmen bought or leased sporting estates in the Highlands, and those natives left were encouraged to take part in activities such as Highland Games. The myth of the 'noble' Highlander was in the making. Yet this was a period of great distress for the poor in the Highlands and Lowlands alike.

The Crimean War of 1854 showed how greatly changed the Highlands really were. The Duke of Sutherland summoned his tenantry to a meeting in Golspie, where 400 or so attended and cheered the Duke politely. He addressed them earnestly on the importance of defeating the Tsar and Russia. Beside him on a table was a heap of gold sovereigns as bounty for recruits, but when he called for volunteers to come forward not a man moved. When he then angrily demanded an explanation, according to Donald McLeod's *Gloomy Memories in the Highlands of Scotland*, an old man came forward and spoke as follows:

I am sorry for the response your Grace's proposals are meeting here today, so near the spot where your maternal grandmother by giving some forty-eight hours notice marshalled 1,500 men to pick out the 800 she required, but there is a cause for it and a genuine cause, and as your Grace demands to know it I must tell you as I see no one else is inclined in the assembly to do so. These lands are now devoted to rear dumb animals which your parents considered of far more value than men. I do assure your Grace that it is the prevailing opinion of this county that, should the Tsar of Russia take possession of Dunrobin Castle and Stafford House next term, we could not expect worse treatment at his hands than we have experienced at the hands of your family for the past fifty years. Your parents, yourself and your Commissioners have desolated the glens and straths of Sutherland where you should find hundreds, yea thousands, of men to meet and respond to your call cheerfully had your parents kept faith with them. How could your Grace expect to find men where they are not and the few of them that are to be found have more sense than to be decoyed like chaff to the field of slaughter? But one comfort you have, though you cannot find men to fight, you can supply those that will fight with plenty of mutton, beef and venison.

In the Crimean War, nevertheless, the Highland regiments distinguished themselves again, fighting and dying in yet another part of the world. The 42nd or Black Watch, the 79th or Cameron Highlanders, and 93rd or Sutherland Highlanders were brigaded together as a single Highland Brigade under General Sir Colin Campbell, later Lord Clyde. At the Battle of Alma on 20 September 1854, the three Highland battalions were given the task of protecting the left flank of the British army. They not only overcame and put to flight eight Russian battalions, the pick of the Russian army, but caused four more to retreat.

On 25 October in the same year, the 93rd Highlanders covered themselves with glory at the Battle of Balaclava. In the words of Surgeon General William Munro, who was with them:

A considerable body of horse wheeling south advanced in our direction at a brisk pace . . . which gradually increased to a gallop . . . The Turkish battalions on our flanks . . . broke and

'The thin red streak tipped with a line of steel' – the 93rd or Sutherland Highlanders standing firm at Balaclava, 1854.

bolted. It was at this moment that Sir Colin Campbell rode along the front of the 93rd telling the Regiment to be 'Steady!' for if necessary every man would have 'to die where he stood.' He was answered by the universal and cheery response, 'Ay, ay, Sir Colin, need's be, we'll do that.'

In the event the 93rd, spread out only two deep, with bayonets fixed, stood firm to the admiration of all who witnessed the battle. The cavalry, faced with two devastating volleys at close range, swerved away and galloped back to their lines in full retreat. In the words of a war correspondent the 93rd were, 'The thin red streak, tipped with a line of steel' – thereafter more frequently known as the 'Thin Red Line'. They were the only infantry regiment to have the word Balaclava on their battle honours.

The Highland Brigade, which fought so well in the Crimea under Sir Colin Campbell, was to find itself transferred direct to India in 1857 on the outbreak of the Indian Mutiny. There it was reunited with its old commander and again performed prodigies of valour. At the relief of Lucknow alone, the 42nd Black Watch and the 93rd Sutherland Highlanders between them gained fifteen VCs.

Meanwhile in 1852 the Highlands and Islands Emigration Society had been formed to provide passages for needy Highlanders to both Canada and Australia. By the time it was wound up, in 1859, the Society had assisted somewhere around 5,000 Highlanders to emigrate. During the 1840s and 1850s very considerable numbers of near-destitute Highlanders were also assisted to emigrate by their landlords. Although rooted in legend and modern mythology, the evidence that evictions, or Clearances, were responsible for any very significant number of emigrants is sadly lacking. On the contrary, it is clear that many landlords, moved by the plight of their tenants, subsidized their passages without hope of any repayment.

By 1856 the colonies were vying with each other to attract emigrants. Amongst much official propaganda to entice the prospective emigrant, J. H. Grant wrote in 1856: 'Canada is no longer a new province with little means of absorbing labour.' He emphasized that emigrants might readily:

> become independent farmers owning 100 or 200 acres of excellent land and enjoying as much real independence as can well fall to the lot of man . . . It is the nearest of our Colonies, and the consequent cheapness of the voyage recommends it . . . With a healthy bracing climate, a soil which produces all the crops raised in this country, land so cheap and so easily attainable that every industrious man may become a freeholder, unsurpassed means of communication through its rivers and lakes, and a greater degree of security than can be enjoyed in any other British colony . . .

In the Highlands, the new landlords replacing the old were mostly English. The steady erosion of Gaelic was continuing apace. In the schools it was still regarded as secondary to English and English was taught without regard to Gaelic's being the native language of many Highlanders. The kilt, if now worn at all, tended to be kept for special days and holidays rather than used every day. Osgood Mackenzie, in his book *A Hundred Years in the*

Highlands, deplored the fact that so many landlords were educated in the south and remained outside their estates except when they wished to indulge in sport. The day of the absentee landlord had arrived. It was scarcely surprising that increasingly the young in the Highlands wished to emigrate.

Quite apart from North America, Australia and New Zealand also offered potent attractions and appealed to many Scots. There was, in addition, still the challenge of India, and also of Africa, which had a particular appeal for some adventurous spirits. Other Scots were to be found in Russia, the Far East, in China, and even further afield. Yet others were exploring South America. The world was still a place of interest to Scots, apparently beckoning them to seek their fortunes. Wherever they might go, they were almost certain to find some emigrant Scots had arrived before them.

5

From 1875 to 1975,
the downward cycle

The latter half of the nineteenth century and the first quarter of the twentieth saw no fewer than seven Scottish Prime Ministers in office: Lord Aberdeen in 1854, followed in due course by William Gladstone, then by Lord Rosebery, Arthur James Balfour, Henry Campbell-Bannerman, Andrew Bonar Law and finally Ramsay Macdonald. It was the period that saw Great Britain at the zenith of her power, epitomized perhaps by the proclamation in 1876 of Queen Victoria as Queen Empress. It was also, conversely, the period that saw Scotland at the nadir of her fortunes, although famed for her ships and engineers from Clydeside, for her whisky, and for her mountain scenery, the playground of rich, English, absentee, Highland landlords.

In Scotland itself the achievements of Scots in the fields of medicine and surgery continued to prove Scottish medical teaching pre-eminent. In the literary field, however, the shining light of Robert Louis Stevenson was to be followed by J. M. Barrie, and by the so-called 'kailyard' school of writers, noted for their 'pawky' characterization and stereotyped speech.

Economic pressures and sheer frustration were still among the strongest reasons causing Scots to emigrate. The disastrous collapse of the City of Glasgow Bank in 1876, for instance, had repercussions throughout the West of Scotland. The Bank had large property interests in Australia and New Zealand, so that one ironic result was no doubt that many ruined by its collapse ended by finding a new life in the very areas where their money had been invested.

The principal casualty in Scotland at this period was the Lowland farming economy. The Lowland Scots had proved excellent farmers, and in the farming boom of the 1860s and early '70s had built themselves fine farmsteadings and buildings. With the influx of cheap grain from the American mid-West in the 1870s, however and later the introduction of refrigerated beef and lamb from the Argentine and the Antipodes, the farming economy slumped badly. Once-rich Lowland farmers now found it hard to scrape a living, and marginal hill-farms were barely worth the rabbits that grazed on them. Inevitably, many of the farmers and their sons emigrated: some may well have taken advantage of the assisted passages to New Zealand instituted in 1871 – the first of such schemes which were to become a feature of the early twentieth century.

A considerable number of Lowland farmers moved south into England to take over farms vacated by Englishmen similarly affected by the farming depression. In East Anglia, especially, many Ayrshire farmers accustomed to a lower standard of living took over farms which their English counterparts had found uneconomic. Since many of these involved a milk round, they were usually close to a town, and subsequently, with the increase in building-land values, became worthwhile assets. After some fifty years or so the Scottish investment in England proved to be a very valuable one, but at the time it merely meant fewer mouths to feed in Scotland.

By 1881 the Cardwell Reforms of the British Army had effected a series of far-reaching changes, not least among the Scottish Highland regiments. Owing largely to the economic conditions already noted, there simply were no longer sufficient Highland recruits available or willing to come forward for the large number of Highland regiments which had been raised in the past. By the simple process of amalgamation the Highland regiments were reduced by the Cardwell Reforms to a total of six, allowing each a selected recruiting area to which it had to adhere. Thus the remnants of the eighty-six Highland regiments which had been recruited between 1730 and 1815 became the Black Watch, the Gordons, the Seaforths, the Camerons, the Highland Light Infantry, and the Argyll and Sutherlands. The percentage of Gaelic-speaking privates or officers in these six remaining Highland regiments was predictably extremely small – in most cases, less than a platoon.

On the other hand the percentage of Scots in high places throughout England and the Empire, especially at this period, should not be underestimated. In professional posts, as lawyers, as doctors and surgeons, in the army and the navy, as well as in the civil service, including particularly the Indian civil service – quite apart from politics – Scots were to be found in the front ranks. It is for example fairly typical that when General Gordon was killed at Khartoum in 1885, the man many claimed as responsible for his death, owing to sheer lack of action at the vital moment, was another Scot (although admittedly second-generation in England) William Gladstone, the Prime Minister.

During the 1880s Scotch whisky began to attain world-wide fame for the first time. The deadly beetle *Phylloxera vastatrix* had attacked the French vineyards in the 1870s, with the result that by the 1880s there was little or no brandy available in Europe. This was the opportunity for Scotch-whisky salesmen of high calibre, such as James Buchanan, later Lord Woolavington, of Black and White fame, and the equally well known Dewar brothers, to make Scotch whisky a household drink. Sales of blended Scotch whisky were soon booming in the south, and then around the world.

Although the Scotch whisky boom came to an abrupt end in the late 1890s with the Pattison brothers' bankruptcy owing to fraudulent business practice, the drink itself was by then well on its way to becoming Scotland's most important export. Already the Distillers Company Limited, better known as the DCL, one of the principal combines in the Scotch whisky industry, had become a company of international renown with far wider interests than those of whisky alone. Throughout the world, Scotch whisky was becoming synonymous with Scotland. Whenever Scots met overseas they were likely to demand their favourite Scotch. No other drink has ever become quite so firmly associated with a nation.

In the Highlands, the 'Highland inn' catering for fishermen, stalkers, or grouse shooters, was by this time becoming a common phenomenon. The Highland estates themselves were changing hands with monotonous frequency, and very few of the original clan chieftains survived without diluting their blood so often, with American heiresses or others, that they could barely qualify as Scots, let alone as Highlanders. Osgood Mackenzie (see p. 71) instanced several cases of newcomers to the Highlands with no Scots blood taking to the kilt and even sometimes learning Gaelic. By now the few Gaelic-speakers left were mostly to be found in the Islands, or on the coastal fringe of the north.

The Queen's Jubilee of 1887 and Diamond Jubilee of 1897 were swiftly followed by the outbreak of the Boer War, when

Britain was sadly humbled on the battlefield by the Boers. The Scots had already made their mark in Africa: Mungo Park and Dr Livingstone had shown that the spirit of the wandering Scot was very much alive, and, as merchants as well as missionaries, the Scots had been successful in opening up new lands and gaining the confidence of the natives.

During the Boer War for the first time the British brought in colonial troops, and soon contingents from Canada, New Zealand, and Australia arrived to fight. Already the Scots were well represented by various Highland and Lowland Scottish regiments, and amongst the colonial forces no doubt there were also many of Scots descent. Inefficient generalship meant that it took three years to bring about a peaceful settlement and there were numerous casualties on both sides.

The death of Queen Victoria and the accession of Edward VII saw not only the end of the century, but also of a state of mind. The world was passing from the nineteenth to the twentieth century, and the change was a radical one; not only from the horse to jet propulsion, from steam to nuclear fission, but from global exploration to adventure in outer space. The world had taken on an entirely new dimension. New conceptions, new inventions, new ways of living constantly followed one another, as the pace of life quickened frenetically. In almost all of these changes Scots played a considerable part, even if Scotland herself had only a minor role.

For Scotland's greatest export still remained the Scots themselves. During the nineteenth century more Scots emigrated to the USA than elsewhere, although Canada, Australia, and New Zealand were also popular. There were variations, but the overall figures remained remarkably constant – for instance, in each decade between 1891 and 1921, the numbers of residents in Australia who had been born in Scotland remained closely around the 100,000 mark.

The Edwardian period from 1901 to 1910 was perhaps the heyday of Britain's greatness. It is possibly significant that the bulk of the period (from 1902 to 1905 and 1905 to 1908) saw two Scots prime ministers, A. J. Balfour and Sir Henry Campbell-Bannerman. The first was the epitome of the social dilettante; the second was a kindly, wise, and patient leader of a brilliant team of individualists. Each in his way was typical of the period, but it is doubtful if either could have done much to prevent the holocaust that was to come.

The 1914–18 Great War was warfare on a scale hitherto unknown. The dominions joined with Britain to fight the Germans and their allies, and instead of opposing forces measured in thousands, for the first time nations opposed each other with forces counted in millions. The war was fought in new elements, in the air and under water, and with new weapons, on a scale never dreamed of before. The life-blood of a generation was drained away.

Nevertheless, with the war Scotland was to some extent revitalized. Her shipyards on the Clyde were working at full pressure, producing ships to replace those sunk by the U-boats. Her farms were doing their best to feed as many as possible to take the load off the hard-pressed shipping. The distilleries were no longer at work, but the distillers were manufacturing munitions or turning to agriculture. Once again, Scots filled the Highland and Lowland regiments with their many proud battle-honours: the Royal Scots alone had thirty battalions during the war. In her sustained efforts to help win the war, Scotland regained much of her old pride in herself.

From all corners of the globe, as well as from Scotland herself, Scots came to join in the war. American Scots, Canadian Scots, Australian Scots, New Zealand Scots, and South African Scots were all represented, as well as many others. The names of the Canadian-Scottish regiments themselves run like a proud roll of honour (see p. 127). To these may be added others from the dominions, such as the New South Wales Scottish, the New Zealand Scottish, and the Transvaal Scottish, to name only a few. There were, of course, honourable exceptions – such as Joseph Hislop, the world-famous tenor, who had taken Swedish citizenship some years earlier to train at the Swedish Opera House and was already well into his thirties. He, however, was amply represented by three younger brothers on the Western front.

With the return of peace, disillusionment was not slow to set in, particularly in Scotland. Farming, which had boomed during the war, relapsed into pre-war slump conditions as soon as cheap imported grain was once again readily available. Clydeside was at first busy replacing the ships sunk during the war, but there, too, it was not long before the yards were silent once again. The introduction of Prohibition by the United States of America in 1920 meant that the whisky distillers, closed during the war, were brought almost to a standstill, and many were forced to close down either temporarily or permanently, with resulting unemployment.

After the war Canada, Australia, New Zealand, and South Africa all participated in a scheme to provide free passages for ex-servicemen (or women), their widows and dependants, from the United Kingdom. By 1922 some 86,000 people had taken advantage of this arrangement for free passage, at a total cost of £2,500,000. In 1922 the Empire Settlement Act was introduced, providing assisted passages for emigrants to Canada, Australia, and New Zealand. Under this Act, Canada provided reduced fares, especially for men with agricultural experience.

In 1924 the Canadian government went further and advanced money for the settlement of families on farms in Canada. This had a familiar sound about it, reminiscent of the original 'plantations' in Virginia, Ulster, and elsewhere. In 1927 the Canadian government called for farm workers, again offering assisted passages. Thus from 1920 to 1929, emigrants from Britain averaged around 50,000 a year.

The Australian government also provided assisted passages for approved emigrants, as did the New Zealand government under the Empire Settlement Act. In 1925 the Australian government agreed to a Migration and Settlement scheme with Britain, to assist the settlement of some 45,000 UK emigrants. Between 1924 and 1928 the average number of emigrants from Britain to Australia was around 35,000, thereafter dropping sharply. In all, the figures for emigration from Scotland, in the decade from 1921 to 1931, were more than half as much again as those of the previous decade; 391,903 as opposed to 238,587.

In Britain the General Strike of 1926 was followed shortly by the slump of 1929 and the depression and bitter unemployment of the 1930s. During the 1930s the depression in the United States, and throughout the world, seems to have slowed up the numbers emigrating considerably, even sending back to Scotland some who had emigrated in the hope of better conditions and had found the future in their prospective country bleaker than at home. By comparison with past figures, for instance, there was virtually no emigration to Canada by Scots from 1929 until 1945; and in Scotland there was some slight sign of economic recovery during this period. Since there was no census in 1941, owing to the War, there can be no certainty about it, but it does seem highly likely that the emigration figures were lower than those in the previous decades.

Even so, the numbers leaving Scotland for one reason or another were still very large by comparison with the population. England, as ever, proved a considerable magnet for many simply because of its accessibility. Many Scots in their inter-war years, for example, took temporary posts in England as domestic servants, as policemen, or in similar occupations, so that they could return home annually for their holidays, possibly marrying and settling down in Scotland at a later date. Others, of course must have settled permanently in England, or moved further afield. The 1931 census revealed that those living in England who had been born in Scotland numbered 366,486. In the same period, the figures for the whole of the United States of America were only 352,323. Of course how many of those Scots in England went on from there to emigrate elsewhere, or to take administrative (or similar) jobs in the British Empire, or dominions, cannot be known.

In the inter-war years, in the 1920s and '30s, there were again two Scottish Prime Ministers. The first, Andrew Bonar Law, was in fact an emigrant Scot – born in Canada, the son of emigrant Scottish parents, he later returned to this country. Entering politics, he reached Cabinet rank but was forced to retire through illness. He recovered to some extent, but was still a sick man when he took office as Prime Minister in 1922, after leading a revolt against Lloyd George's coalition government. In the event, Bonar Law resigned for health reasons in 1923 and died soon afterwards.

Ramsay Macdonald, born in 1886 at Lossiemouth, near Elgin, was a remarkable tribute to the results of Scottish education. His father was a ploughman, John Macdonald, who never married his mother, Anne Ramsay. His mother, however, managed to find the 8d a month required to send him to Drainie school, where at the age of sixteen he became a pupil teacher. He first stood for Parliament in 1895 for the Independent Labour Party. In 1896 he married a rich wife, and thereafter his monetary troubles were solved. In 1906 he was elected to Parliament as a Labour Party member, but his wife's death in 1911 was a considerable blow to him. In 1918 he lost his seat.

In 1922 he was elected to Parliament once more and became Parliamentary leader of the Labour Party. In 1924 he became Prime Minister, but his government failed to last a year when he tried to institute friendly relations with the Communist government of Russia. Returned to office in 1929, his cabinet split in 1931 on economic policy, and he formed a Nationalist government which lasted until 1935.

In the last few years before the outbreak of the 1939–1945 World War, there was something of an economic upsurge in Scotland. The yards on Clydeside once again sounded to the hammers of riveters, as orders for new warships were belatedly made. Other industries, jute and heavy engineering, also bene-fited from Government orders.

During the Second World War Scots from all round the world once more took up arms to fight for freedom. This time, however, Tiger Clemenceau's epic words on the kilt were remembered: *'Pour l'amour bon, pour la guerre, non!'* The kilt, which had proved to be a considerable handicap against barbed-wire, was not worn in combat officially, although still worn by pipers and bandsmen and on ceremonial duties.

Clydeside and the industrial belt of Scotland geared them-selves to producing ships and munitions for the war effort; the rich farmlands of the Lowlands turned again to producing food for the population of the British Isles. In 1942 a Scottish Conven-tion was formed for 'Scottish reform . . . to express the will of the Scottish people', but at such a time of national crisis it made little impact.

The spirit of national unity which prevailed throughout the war unfortunately did not last long into the peace which followed, with the advent of a Socialist government in June 1945. When a Scottish National Party candidate, Dr Robert McIntyre, was elected at a by-election for Motherwell in the April preceding the General Election, it was regarded as an electoral freak, but in the decades thereafter the stirrings of nationalism became stronger, as discontent grew with centralized, ineffective, and inefficient government in the south.

Farming was not allowed to slump as it had done after the

previous war, for in the cheerless post-war years of austerity and restrictions, of rationing and gloom, it became even more important to grow as much food as possible than it had been during the war. It even became necessary to introduce bread-rationing, which had never happened in the worst days of wartime. Restrictions on essentials such as steel and coal held back production in factories and shipyards. The general picture in Scotland, as in England, was gloomy in the extreme, with demobilized ex-servicemen unable to find jobs and impatient at restrictions. In such circumstances it is scarcely surprising that many decided to emigrate, but there were restrictions on this too, so that it was no longer as simple as it had been before the war.

In 1947 India was given independence, with the partition of India and Pakistan as separate states. The scuttle to get rid of an Empire followed during the years of Socialist rule. In almost every instance, independence was followed by uprisings, revolutions, and ultimately by dictatorships.

One effect of this dismemberment of an Empire was that many young Scots who would otherwise have gone abroad to govern, administer, advise, or assist some part of the Empire were now forced to find their living at home. The endless drain of good brains and restless spirits into the maw of the Empire was over at last. The result of this was, of course, emigration on the one hand, but on the other, a fresh outlook in Scotland itself, with new developments, new industries, and new towns. The gradual rebirth of nationalism was another natural side-effect.

A table of the total number of emigrants from the United Kingdom in 1948 and 1949 is of interest, as is the small but already noticeable increase in immigrants over the same period:

	1948	1949
Total emigrated from UK	157,209	144,503
To Australia	34,445	53,059
To Canada	34,487	20,762
To New Zealand	6,927	9,261
To South Africa	27,726	11,367
To Rhodesia	4,506	3,916
To the United States	19,600	16,237
Immigrants to the UK	53,034	59,397

In 1947 the Scottish Convention, which had been founded in 1942, formed a Scottish National Assembly, a non-party body of some 600 delegates from various political parties, local authorities, churches, trade unions, co-operative societies, and similar bodies. In 1949, at their third session, the National Assembly adopted a Covenant which read: 'We, the people of Scotland who subscribe this Engagement declare our belief that reform in the Constitution of our country is necessary to secure good government . . . We affirm that the desire for such reform is both deep and widespread . . . we pledge ourselves . . . to secure for Scotland a Parliament with adequate legislative authority in Scottish affairs.' By 1950, more than a million signatures had been secured for this Covenant.

A committee on Scottish Financial and Trade Statistics appointed by the government in 1950 under the Chairmanship of Lord Catto, a former Governor of the Bank of England, submitted a report in 1952 recommending the appointment of a Royal Commission. Accordingly the government, by this time once more Conservative, set up a Royal Commission for Scottish Affairs, 'To review, with reference to the financial, economic, administrative, and other considerations involved, the arrangements for exercising the functions of H M Government in relation to Scotland and to report.'

The Chairman of this Royal Commission was the third Earl of Balfour, who had served as Chairman of the Scottish Coal Board. It is possibly worth noting that he was a great-great-grandson of James Balfour of Whittingehame, the nabob, (see p. 63) and a nephew of A. J. Balfour, the Prime Minister and first Earl. During his chairmanship of the Scottish Coal Board, the new town of Glenrothes in Fife was built as a special miners' town, with new pit-head baths and every facility, at a cost of a million pounds. By a strange quirk of fate it was sited next to the Balbirnie estate of James Balfour of Whittingehame's brother. Only after it was completed was it discovered that the coal seams beneath it were exhausted. It is perhaps because the town then had to attract its own industry that it subsequently developed into one of the most prosperous of the new towns built in post-war Scotland.

The other members of the Commission were the usual government appointees. Mr C. W. Guillebaud, a Fellow of St John's College, Cambridge, was the economics adviser, and had served on several other Conservative-appointed boards and commissions. Although not a Scot, it might at least be argued in his favour that he was not a Hungarian.

The report of the Royal Commission, when published in 1954, stated that since its terms of reference excluded consideration of parliamentary devolution, the Commissioners had sought no evidence in this connection, but they noted the 'strong views' of various witnesses on the subject. 'The "substantial majority" of these bodies – including the Convention of Royal Burghs, the Association of County Councils, the Scottish representatives of the CBI and the TUC General Council – had strongly opposed the creation of a separate Scottish Parliament.' Accordingly the Commissioners merely made five minor recommendations for the transfer of governmental control from London, chiefly to the Secretary for Scotland. Like any good Royal Commission, it had come up with what Parliament wanted to hear.

Meanwhile, with the Korean War from 1950 to 1953 and continued national service, the country remained in a state of uneasy peace. The period of the Cold War with Russia and the satellite Soviet States continued well into the 1960s, on a global scale. The advent of the uranium bomb and then the first men in space in 1961 and 1962 (Yuri Gagarin in 1961 and John Glenn, of Scots descent, in 1962) brought about an entirely new form of Cold Peace, known as co-existence.

Once again, there were two Scottish Prime Ministers in this period. The first, Harold Macmillan, came of crofting stock, but his grandfather had founded the famous publishing firm. The second, Sir Alec Douglas-Home, who gave up his title as the fourteenth Earl of Home to take office, and finally reverted to the House of Lords as Lord Home, was of long-standing Border stock. Both were Conservatives and neither favoured Scottish Nationalism.

It is only fair to add that no political party in Parliament favoured Scottish Nationalism during the 1960s, or indeed in the early 1970s. It was not until 1967 that Mrs Winfred Ewing was elected as SNP member for Hamilton. By 1974 there were two members of the SNP in Parliament and then the numbers rose abruptly to eleven, making it a force to be reckoned with in the later 1970s.

The discovery of North Sea oil and its development in the

1970s was one of the major planks of the Scottish National Party, along with the demand for devolution. The cry was that 'Scottish oil should be used for Scotland's benefit' and that a Scottish Parliament should meet in Edinburgh. With eleven members in Parliament, the SNP pressed even harder for devolution of power from London to Edinburgh. Yet however much the Scots desired some decentralization of government from London, the referendum of 1979 returned a decisive negative to devolution. In this respect the SNP had already served its turn, for Scotland regained a national pride which had been very nearly lost, submerged beneath Whitehall red-tape and government-from-a-distance. The fact that the SNP is always waiting in the wings is now a sufficient spur to politicians to pay full attention to Scottish matters.

The number of Scots emigrating during the post-war period remained fairly constant, limited by various factors. The Social Security contributions and benefits provided by the State since the 1950s have, to some, been a disincentive to emigration, although those so-minded are, of course, the very ones least likely to consider emigration in the first place. Conversely, the better terms offered by New Zealand's National Insurance scheme were at one time an incentive to those who considered this a matter of first importance. Lack of opportunities for individuals in Scotland and an overall feeling of restriction and frustration, along with over-high taxation, definitely encouraged emigration. Assisted passages to New Zealand and Australia also helped.

The loss of incentive in Britain for engineers, nuclear physicists, electronic experts, and senior managers, amongst others, led to what has been termed the 'brain drain' throughout the later 1960s and '70s. Taxation reached the stage in Britain where there was a positive disincentive to save, or to aim at promotion where financial returns were increasingly in inverse proportion to the work and responsibility involved. Looking abroad, senior executives saw their opposite numbers rewarded on a far higher scale, and naturally many of them left the country.

When Britain joined the Common Market there was no increased incentive to stay in this country; indeed rather the reverse. Skilled artisans were offered higher wages in Europe for their particular skills as (for example) electricians, engineers, or builders. The high wages and tax-free benefits offered, not only on the Continent and in oil-rich Arab States but in Africa as well, certainly attracted many Scots overseas during this period, and continue to do so in the 1980s.

One of the few countries which has not attracted many Scots, or indeed emigrants from any other country, since the 1917 Revolution, is, of course, Soviet Russia. While, as has been noted, the Scots attained considerable power and influence at many periods in Russian history, since 1917 there has been none of the freedom of expression which the Scots require. It is thus mildly ironic that in modern Russia, as in Japan, there is very consider-able admiration for the poetry of Robert Burns, that ardent advocate of freedom, and Burns Clubs are to be found flourishing in both these countries. On Burns Nights there the national bard of Scotland is quoted with all the fervour normally only to be found amongst Scots themselves, when whisky and Burns are freely mixed in national celebration.

It is remarkable that the Scots have survived at all as a nation, and it is even more remarkable how they have spread themselves around the world. That they have survived so many vicissitudes in their history is a matter for pride. The sheer numbers of those with Scottish ancestry around the world is also something in which the Scots may take pride. The deep ties Scotland has with emigrant Scots is one of her unseen, but most powerful and valuable, assets.

Numerous Scottish Clan and Family Societies have repre-sentatives in local branches around the world who keep in touch with each other through regular news-letters. Many towns, es-pecially the Border towns with their annual Common Ridings, regularly welcome back expatriates, and there is hardly an issue of a local newspaper in Scotland without mention of returned exiles, or news of emigrant Scots.

When the first International Clan Gathering was held in Edinburgh in May 1977, there was a very positive response from overseas. Scots gathered from Australia, Canada, New Zealand, and the United States of America, as well as from places as diverse as Mexico, Sweden, and Japan. The Scots themselves were possibly somewhat surprised by the numbers of overseas Scots who attended this Gathering. With the Scots habit of poking fun at themselves, it was easy to find humour in the sight of Mayor Lindsay of New York leading a kilted parade of Australians, Canadians, and New Zealanders through Edinburgh in a typical Scottish drizzle. Yet it was in truth a subject for pride, and it was repeated in 1981, with the prospect of becoming a regular event. Scots both at home and abroad should support such gatherings with pride and humility, for they represent a past in which Scotland triumphed over adversity, and a present when emigrant Scots acknowledge their debt to their ancestors. It is a visible reminder of Scotland's worldwide heritage.

PART II

Arrival and impact:
The emigrant Scots

6

The United States of America

After the American War of Independence from 1775 to 1783, came the difficult and lengthy task of evolving a Constitution and a form of government agreeable to the various states. Amongst Americans of Scottish descent in the convention which met to agree on the new Constitution, were James Wilson from Pennsylvania, William S. Johnson from Connecticut, Alexander Hamilton from New York, and William Paterson from New Jersey. In February 1789 Congress elected George Washington and John Adams the first President and Vice-President of the Thirteen States of the Union, then consisting of (in order of joining) Delaware, Pennsylvania, New Jersey, Georgia, Connecticut, Massachusetts, Maryland, South Carolina, New Hampshire, Virginia, New York, North Carolina, and Rhode Island.

At this time the bulk of the country was agricultural and very few industries had begun to be established. There were only five cities with populations of over 10,000, namely New York (33,000), Philadelphia (28,000), Boston (18,000), Charleston (16,000), and Baltimore (13,000). By the first census of 1790, the total population of the United States was estimated at only some 4 million, including something over half a million black slaves, but not including the Indians whose numbers no one could estimate accurately.

According to this 1790 census there were 189,000 people of Scottish origin in the United States. On the other hand, between 1720 and 1790 it is estimated that some 200,000 people of Scottish descent had emigrated from Ulster. It is probable, therefore, that many of these Ulster Scots, or Scots-Irish, as they were known, made up the figures in this census.

Major-General Alexander Hamilton, Secretary of the Treasury, and Henry Knox, Secretary of War, both of Scottish parentage, were prominent in the new government, which included Thomas Jefferson as Secretary of State. At Hamilton's prompt-

At the inauguration of General George Washington as first President of
the United States, 1789, the military escort was commanded by Brigadier General William Malcolm, the kilted figure in the centre.

ing, very early on the principle of tariff protection was established
as a cornerstone of the United States economic policy, and
foreign imports were expected to pay up to 10 per cent duty. Nor
was it long before Washington established, as a guiding principle
in foreign affairs, that the President should seek neutrality
whenever possible.

In 1793 Eli Whitney invented the new cotton gin, as a result of
which it became possible for one slave to produce 1,000 lbs of
cotton a day instead of a mere six lbs. The exports of cotton
consequently rose, from 189,000 lbs in 1791 to 21,000,000 lbs in
1801. In the same decade Vermont (1791), Kentucky (1792), and
Tennessee (1796) were all admitted to the Union, while the
population of Ohio rose from practically nothing to 15,000; that
of Tennessee from 36,000 to 106,000; and that of Kentucky from

74,000 to 221,000. The movement to the West had just begun, but the vast expansion and population movements of the mid-century were still to come.

In 1880 Thomas Jefferson became President, with Aaron Burr (of Scots descent) as Vice President, after a disputed election decided in the newly chosen capital city of Washington, to which the government had removed from Philadelphia. In 1803 came the 'Louisiana Purchase' by which Louisiana was bought for $15,000,000 from Napoleon, who had acquired it from Spain. By this means, control of the great river systems of central North America came under the direction of the United States government.

In 1804 the mutual dislike between Aaron Burr and Alexander Hamilton finally culminated in a duel in which the latter was killed but by which the former ruined himself. Although both of Scots descent, each was the antithesis of the other. Hamilton, an excellent judge of men, had done his best to block the other at every opportunity, both in the army and in politics, while at the bar they were bitter rivals. Each was a member of the New York St Andrew's Society, although Hamilton appears to have been much the more popular. In the Society's history it is noted that they both 'attended the St Andrew's Day Banquet prior to their duel, and Hamilton, on invitation, sang a song'. It is significant that subsequently the members erected a monument to Hamilton's memory but Burr appears to have been ostracized.

The St Andrew's Society of New York, although founded in 1756, was in effect the successor to the Scots Society of New York founded in 1744, which ceased in 1754. The St Andrew's Society of Philadelphia was founded in 1749, while that of Charleston was as early as 1729. All, of course, were ante-dated by the Charitable Society founded by the Scots in Boston in 1657, but the principle behind them remained the same, although as the years passed they tended to become regular dining-clubs as well as charitable organizations.

Many other Scottish societies, such as Burns Clubs, Scots Friendly Societies, and Caledonian Societies were also formed. The first Burns Club in New York dates from about 1820. At about that time there were also a good number of inns and taverns in New York with a decidedly Scottish flavour – for example, the Burns Tavern, at 2 Liberty Street; the Blue Bonnet at 10

The menu for the anniversary banquet of the St Andrew's Society of New York State, held in 1856.

Frankfort Street; the Ram's Head at 122 Fulton Street; and the Rob Roy House at Greenwich and Hammond Streets. It would appear that the Scots in New York had plenty of choice if they wanted a dram with a fellow countryman.

In 1804 Jefferson was re-elected, being followed by James Madison as President in 1809. Two further states admitted to the Union about this time were Ohio (1802) and Louisiana (1812). In the same year, 1812, a Scot, John Bradbury, among the first to visit the Missouri valley, published a book entitled *Travels in the interior of America in 1809, 1810 and 1811*. Primarily a naturalist, John Bradbury was fortunate in falling in with three experienced fellow Scots going the same way: Wilson P. Hunt, of Scottish origins, Ramsay Crooks, born at Greenock in 1787, and Donald Mackenzie, a relative of Sir Alexander Mackenzie, the explorer. Bradbury wrote:

> On my return to St Louis, I was informed that a party of men had arrived from Canada, with an intention to ascend the Missouri on their way to the Pacific Ocean (by the same route that Lewis and Clarke had followed) by descending the Columbia River. I soon became acquainted with the principals of this party, in whom the manners and accomplishments of gentlemen were united with the hardihood and capability of suffering of the backwoodsman. As they were apprised of the nature and object of my mission, Mr Wilson P. Hunt, the leader of the party, in a very kindly and pressing manner, invited me to accompany them up the river Missouri as far as might be agreeable to my views ... I gladly accepted the invitation, to which an acquaintance with Messrs Ramsay Crooks and Donald M'Kenzie, also principals of the party, was no small inducement ...

It was in the year 1812, during his second term in office, that President Madison found himself committed to declaring war on Britain. John C. Calhoun and William H. Crawford, both of whom had Scottish antecedents, were amongst the new young advisors who resented the British navy's high-handed treatment of United States shipping during the blockade of Europe. They expected Canada to rise in revolt also, but the Canadians proved to be strong Loyalists. In 1812 General Hill was forced to surrender at Detroit, and in 1814 Washington was burned by British troops. American honour was saved by the successful repulse of a British attack on Louisiana, just prior to the announcement of peace in 1815.

The war and blockade were an active form of protection under which American manufacturers flourished, but with the return of peace British manufacturers soon drove most of their American competitors out of business. There was, however, rapid industrialization in the United States and in 1816 a tariff of 25 per cent was imposed on cotton and woollen goods.

In 1816 James Monroe was elected President in succession to Madison, and was re-elected with virtually no opposition in 1820, serving until 1824. His father, Spence Monroe, had been an early eighteenth-century Scottish settler; he himself was born in 1758 at Monroe's Creek, a tributary of the Potomac in Westmoreland, Virginia, named after his father. Here was a typical example of a place named after a Scot – as, for instance, Paterson town in Putnam County of New York was named after Matthew Paterson who settled there in the eighteenth century. Other examples proliferate throughout the United States.

Monroe's period in office has been termed 'the era of good feeling'. It included the successful Seminole War (1817–18), the agreement on the 49th Parallel as the border with Canada as far as the Oregon territory (1818), the acquisition of the Floridas from Spain (1819–21), and the Missouri Compromise of 1820, by which the first official conflict about slavery under the constitution was successfully adjusted.

There were also tremendous developments in the West, owing to the Mississippi steamboats. Indiana was admitted as a new state in 1816, followed by Mississippi (1817), Illinois (1818), Alabama (1819), Maine (1820), and Missouri (1821). All, excepting Maine, were the result of westward expansion. Illinois, in particular, owed much to a Scot, Morris Birkbeck, whose *Notes on a Journey from the West Coast of Virginia to the territory of Illinois*, published in 1817, and subsequent *Letters from Illinois*, were good publicity for the area.

It was Monroe who first demonstrated the weight of American power in North and South America. In 1823 it seemed possible that Spain might be assisted by European allies to try to regain her former American colonies, which had successfully asserted their independence. Canning hinted that Great Britain would not support such a move. In these circumstances the American President formulated what came to be known as the Monroe Doctrine, or Declaration.

He stated: 'We could not view any interposition for the purposes of oppressing them (the South American States) or controlling in any other manner their destiny by any European power in any other light than as the manifestation of an unfriendly disposition towards the United States.' Backed by Great Britain, this stopped the project immediately.

Supposing that Spain might consider transferring her colonial claims to a stronger power, Monroe added: 'The American continents, by the free and independent condition which they have assumed and maintained, are henceforth not to be considered as subjects for future colonization by any European power.' Allied to the already well-established refusal of the United States to become entangled in European wars or alliances, this resulted in increasing American isolationism until 1917.

In 1824 John Quincey Adams was elected President, and in 1828 he was succeeded by Andrew Jackson, with John C. Calhoun as Vice-President. Both the latter were of Scots origin, and both were re-elected for a second term. It was under Jackson that the system of using office as a political weapon on a national scale was developed. The political nomination machinery was also developed during this period, with the opportunities for graft this inevitably involved.

There followed several single-term presidencies: Martin Van Buren, General William H. Harrison (the old Indian War-hero who died of pneumonia and was succeeded abruptly by his Vice-President John Tyler), and James K. Polk. It was during the latter's administration in 1846 that war was declared with Mexico over a border dispute. After a successful campaign by General Zachary Taylor in the north and General Winfield Scott (of Scottish descent) in the south, peace was concluded in 1848.

The peace terms included cession by Mexico of California, Utah, Arizona and New Mexico, on payment by the United States of $15,000,000 and acceptance of $3,000,000-worth of debts due to United States citizens. Meanwhile, in 1846 the north-west boundary between Oregon and British Columbia had been settled by the Webster-Ashburton Treaty. Thus the United States had attained its territorial form, requiring only the annexation of Alaska.

Considering himself ill-used during the Mexican campaign, General Taylor returned home and stood against Martin Van Buren for the presidency, being duly elected and taking office in 1849. In the same year gold was discovered in California, leading to the famous gold rush of that year. In 1850 California was admitted as a state, soon after General Taylor's death at the hands of his physicians and his succession by Vice-President Martin Fillmore.

In 1852 Franklin Pierce, opposing General Winfield Scott, was elected by the political machine. In 1856 he was succeeded by James Buchanan, another President of Scots descent, but, like his predecessor, extremely weak. By this time the gap between north and south was becoming very pronounced, and in 1860, when Abraham Lincoln became President, the country was already poised on the verge of civil war.

There had been, however, thirty years of immense developments and important invention. Cyrus Hall McCormick's reaping-machine in 1834 revolutionized harvesting methods. In 1839 Charles Goodyear invented a method of vulcanizing rubber; in 1846 the sewing-machine and the power-loom were invented, but, more important still, surgical anaesthesia was finally developed in that same year; and in 1847 the first rotary printing press was invented, a device to be much used by journalistic Scots (among others) in the years to follow.

In 1830 there were only twenty-three miles of railway. By 1835 there were 1,098 miles, by 1848 2,800 miles, and thereafter the mileage doubled every five years until 1860. By 1837 the anthracite coal of the middle states was being used on railways and in steelmaking, and the demand for Scots skilled in mining and steelmaking soon grew apace. In 1844 the telegraph was introduced as a result of S. F. B. Morse's invention. Communications were improving all the time and the way to the West was wide open at last.

In 1832 Chicago was only a frontier fort, but by 1838 it was a flourishing town, with eight steamers connecting it with Buffalo. Between 1830 and 1840 the population of Ohio rose from 900,000 to 1,500,000, while that of Michigan rose from 32,000 to 212,000, and that of the United States as a whole from

13,000,000 to 17,000,000. Between 1836 and 1850 seven new states were admitted – Arkansas (1836), Michigan (1837), Florida (1845), Texas (1845), Iowa (1846), Wisconsin (1848), and California, as noted, in 1850. After the Black Hawk War in Iowa and Wisconsin in 1832, and the Seminole War in Florida in 1835–7, the defeated Indians were forced to cede lands in return for peace, and the early admission of Iowa, Wisconsin, and Florida was the direct result.

As late as 1820 the number of immigrants was only 8,000 per year. Until 1842 the annual total never reached 100,000, and it then fell to almost half that number. In 1847, however, it rose to 235,000, and in 1849, after the revolutions of 1848 in Europe, it rose to 300,000, although in 1850 it fell back to 228,000. Between 1847 and 1854, however, more than 2¼ million immigrants from overseas settled in the United States.

Not surprisingly, several books were written about this time giving advice to intending emigrants. One such, published in London in 1849, was entitled *The Emigrants' Guide to the United States. Who should and should not emigrate. Being plain practical advice to intending emigrants*, *by B*. Chapter II, headed 'Those who should emigrate', began: 'First in the list I place farmers, possessed of a small capital, and farm servants, possessed of strong hands and willing hearts. *Those are the people who will get on . . .*'

In 1854 only 4,888 Scots emigrated to the United States, whereas 6,706 went to Canada; but from 1870 to 1900 some 53 per cent of Scots emigrants went to the United States. By 1850 there were almost 5,000 Scots in Illinois alone; in that year there were only 700 in Iowa, but by 1860 there were 3,000. In 1852 an Ayrshire schoolmaster, John Regan, who finally settled in Illinois, wrote *The Emigrant's Guide to the Western States of America*. By 1857 he was proprietor and editor of the *Messenger* in Illinois. In his book he recommended emigration to those prepared to work hard, and instanced a Scots acquaintance named David Crawford, from Linlithgow, who emigrated to Quebec in 1841 at the age of fifty and eventually reached Iowa without a penny to his name. Starting by working in a brickyard, he went on into farming. He married a Scots girl of thirty from Glasgow and soon had two children. By the time he was sixty his capital consisted of '20 acres of good land, good framed house, 2 horses and a wagon, 6 cows, 3 heifers, 4 calves, 30 sheep, and more in prospect, 30 hogs with several litters of young, poultry, turkeys, geese, ducks and hens in swarms. And a little CASH in a quiet corner for a rainy day.' Regan's conclusion was: 'To all who feel themselves pinched and straitened in the old world from no fault of their own, I would say Westward Ho . . .'

There is little doubt that the Scots made up in quality what they may have lacked in quantity. In 1848, for example, a family named Carnegie, consisting of a husband, wife, and two sons, sailed for Pittsburgh from Glasgow. The husband had owned four looms there, but the introduction of the power-loom had brought him to the point of bankruptcy. He had two sisters in Pittsburgh and he decided to join them. In the United States his eldest son, Andrew, started as a bobbin boy, graduating to messenger boy, then telegraphist on the railways, before finally going into the steel business in Pittsburgh. By 1860 he was well on his way to making a spectacular fortune (see p. 105).

In 1858 Minnesota was admitted to the Union, followed by Oregon (1859) and Kansas (1860). By 1860 the population of the United States was over 31 million, an increase of 8 million in ten years. It was a feature of this period of massive immigration that it was almost all in the north and west. As late as 1800 it was notable that, except in Louisiana, Texas, and Florida, there were no foreign elements to be found in the southern states. Until 1845, when Texas was the last slave state admitted, the admission to the Union of a free state had been balanced by that of a slave state, but by 1860 there were nineteen free states against twelve slave states. The north had a population of around 19 million, against 12 million in the south of which 4 million were slaves.

The southern states seceded and prepared for war almost from the moment that Lincoln's election was announced. He had barely taken office before the first clash occurred at Fort Sumter. Fortunately the governors of the northern states were an able group and several of them took it on themselves to order supplies as they saw events moving inexorably towards war. Among those of Scots extraction were Austin Blair of Michigan, Alexander Ramsay of Minnesota, John Albion Andrew of Massachusetts, and Andrew Gregg Curtin of Pennsylvania. Two of the first northern commanders under General Ulysses S. Grant (himself of Scottish descent) were generals Johnston and Gordon – also good Scots names.

The Confederate and Federal forces fought a hard and bitter war until lack of manufactures eventually told against the south. In 1863 West Virginia was admitted as a new state, and the war was mostly fought south of Delaware, Maryland, Kentucky, and Missouri. It became a struggle against slavery, hence although the south was favoured by many outside America there was no overt interference. The victories of Gettysburg and Vicksburg in 1863 turned the scales finally in favour of the north.

A regiment with a decided Scottish flavour, which was raised in the north in 1860 and went to the front in 1861, was the 79th Highlanders of New York. The regimental uniform was the kilt with the Cameron of Erracht tartan, although sometimes trews in the same tartan seem to have been worn. Many of the officers and men of this regiment were also members of the St Andrew's Society of New York. Another regiment with a Scottish background was the Caledonian Fusiliers of New York, who appear to have worn trews. There were, of course, many of Scots descent on either side, although, once again, as in the War of Independence, they were notable amongst the higher ranks, particularly amongst the generals.

In 1864 Lincoln was re-elected with Andrew Johnson (of Scots descent and humbler background) from Tennessee as Vice-President. In 1864 Nevada was admitted as the thirty-ninth State. The following year, on 9 April 1865, General Robert E. Lee surrendered to General Ulysses S. Grant at Appomattox, Virginia. On 26 April General Joseph E. Johnston, the only other Confederate general with any forces left under his command, also surrendered. The Confederate armies were estimated to have been about 700,000 at best, but by the time of their surrender they were reduced to a mere 200,000 while the Federal army amounted to close on a million men. General Grant, however, allowed generous terms and when politicians tried to alter them at a later date he insisted on their being honoured.

Soon after Lee's surrender, President Lincoln was assassinated. Andrew Johnson, intemperate and opinionated, succeeded him. After some slight hesitation, however, Johnson accepted the main principles laid down by Lincoln, providing an amnesty to those who took an oath of loyalty for the future. Virginia, Tennessee, Louisiana, and Arkansas all had governments recognized by Lincoln. By 1865 all the states had formed constitutions and elected governments except Texas, which delayed until 1866, but this was naturally a time of great upheaval in the south.

Men who came into the southern states from outside and stood for office were known as carpet-baggers. White loyalists in the south were known as scalawags. Both were detested by the great majority of southerners. They and the negroes themselves were intimidated by secret societies such as the Ku-Klux-Klan, or the Knights of the White Camellia, who were not above flogging their victims or hanging them. The 'Grand Wizard' of the Klan was General Nathaniel B. Forrest, and General John B. Gordon of Scottish descent (one of Stonewall Jackson's cavalry commanders), was 'Grand Dragon' for Georgia. Although the Klan was officially disbanded in 1869 and the Knights of the White Camellia in 1870, intimidation of the negroes continued in one form or another.

In 1867 Russia offered to sell Alaska to the United States. This was duly accepted by Secretary of State William B. Seward under President Johnson. The purchase price agreed was $7,200,00. In 1868 General U.S. Grant was elected President, largely on the negro vote of the southern states.

This was a time of expansion, recovery, and speculation. The oilfields of Pennsylvania and Ohio, the gold and silver fields in the far West, the protection afforded by tariffs, and the enormous demand for manufacturers, along with the vast consumption of the fast expanding West, resulted in the rapid growth of great fortunes.

It was officially reported in 1869 that in the previous five years more cotton spindles had been put in motion, more iron furnaces erected, more iron smelted, more bars rolled, more steel made, more coal and copper mined, more lumber sawn and hewn, more houses and shops constructed, more manufactories of different kinds started, and more petroleum collected, refined, and exported, than during any equal period in the history of the country. Such claims were not hard to believe.

Throughout the 1850s and '60s Scottish coal-miners had emigrated in considerable numbers, particularly west of the Alleghenies, and were to be found in Maryland and Pennsylvania, and as far west as Illinois and Ohio. The mining town of Braidwood in Illinois, and What Cheer in Iowa, both had large Scottish populations. Wages were so high, however, that quite a number of miners found it profitable enough to work only the summer months in America, either working their sea-passage each way or travelling steerage.

There were also communities of Scottish stonemasons in Maine, New Hampshire, and Massachusetts; and many also worked in the sandstone quarries of Northern Ohio. In the 1860s an American tariff was introduced on imported Aberdeen granite, and the skilled knowledge of Scots stonemasons was at a premium in America – so much so that, as was the case with coal-mining, it was for a time profitable enough to allow annual commuting across the Atlantic.

In the 1860s there was another fast-growing industry in America where Scottish skills could earn considerable return. During the American Civil War the cotton industry in Scotland had suffered a severe recession because of the lack of raw materials, and because of the United States tariffs on imported goods. Scottish workers emigrating to America, where the manufacturing industry had greatly expanded, found they could earn nearly double their wages in Scotland, although they were forced to work much harder.

Two Scottish firms from Paisley, connected with the cotton industry and producing thread for sewing-machines, found it paid them to set up firms in the United States with skilled workers from their Scottish factories. The well-known firm of Coats built a factory at Pawtucket in New Jersey, and the firm of George A. Clark built theirs at Newark. They found they could pay nearly twice the wages offered in Scotland.

Between 1862 and 1872 there was an extraordinary extension of the railways. The Union Pacific and Central Pacific were granted nearly 33,000,000 acres, and a route connecting the East with San Francisco was begun in 1866 and completed in 1869. Between 1868 and 1873 some 500 million dollars were invested and some 28,000 miles added to the railroads.

The advance of the railway had its effects on the far West. The bison were divided into northern and southern herds by the Union Pacific in 1869; the southern herds were slaughtered between 1870 and 1879, and the northern herds between 1880 and 1883. The repeating-carbine and the extinction of the bison resulted in the retreat of the Plains Indians, and the consequent gain of a vast new area of cattle country.

Between 1860 and 1880 the population of the north-central group of states, mainly grain-growing, rose by 8 million. In the same two decades the production of wheat and oats doubled. Between 1870 and 1880 a total area of 300,000 square miles, the equivalent of Great Britain and France combined, was added to the cultivated territory of the United States. A surprising amount of this expansion was financed by Scottish capital, cattle companies in New Mexico, Texas, Colorado, Kansas, Wyoming, Nebraska, and Montana being backed by Scottish banks.

Amongst individual Scots who took advantage of these opportunities were two notable figures. In 1875 John Sutherland Sinclair went out, aged seventeen, and by 1891 was farming in North Dakota in a very big way, before inheriting the title of Earl of Caithness. In 1881 the Earl of Airlie invested heavily in the Prairie Land and Cattle Company and bought a large ranch in Colorado, dying of a heart attack in Denver.

Railway failures in 1873 resulted in a five-year slump when railway-building virtually ceased. As late as 1877, more than 18 per cent of railway mileage was still in the hands of receivers. The iron industry also slumped heavily, and there was a deep depression throughout most industries. The general effect was the ending of many partnerships and individual businesses and their replacement by corporations. President Grant's poor choice of associates led to a considerable amount of maladministration and outright fraud amongst government officials, which resulted in further loss of public confidence.

In 1875 Rutherford B. Hayes of Ohio was elected President. He was followed in 1880 by General James A. Garfield, who was assassinated soon afterwards and succeeded by Vice-President Chester A. Arthur of Scots descent. He in turn was followed by Grover Cleveland, the Governor of New York, in 1884. Cleveland was beaten at the polls in 1888 by General Benjamin Harrison, ineffectual grandson of the Indian War hero General William H. Harrison (see p. 95). Cleveland had his revenge in 1892 when he in turn defeated Harrison.

Between 1880 and 1890 the population grew from 50 million to more than 62 million. With the increase in population and the growth in industry, the necessity to import skilled workers decreased. During the 1870s Scottish expertise in the iron and steel industry was no longer required, and in the 1880s the need for more Scots in the coal-mines ceased, but it was as late as 1900 before the American textile industry could dispense with further Scottish assistance and direction. To some extent this caused a slowing-up of emigration from Scotland after 1900.

The reason for America's colossal population explosion was the burst of railway-building when the 1873 panic was over. Pioneers pushed into Nebraska and the west of Kansas: Nebraska's population grew from 123,000 in 1870 to nearly half a million in 1880; that of Kansas from a third of a million in 1870 to a million by 1880 and nearly 1½ million by 1890. A cycle of abundant rains seemed to prove the Great American Desert a myth; but after 1886 drought and grasshoppers soured the high hopes of the settlers, and Kansas lost almost a seventh of its population. It was fully a decade before prosperity returned.

The Chicago railroads pushed on into Iowa, Minnesota, and the Dakotas, where virgin prairie provided wonderful wheat crops. The older wheat areas were thus forced to diversify, and with the newly invented roller-mills, Minneapolis became a great flour-milling centre. In the same period, the pine forests of Michigan, Wisconsin, and Minnesota were exploited by means of the railroads.

The Great Northern railroad (the personal project of James J. Hill, with the backing of Scots Canadians Norman Kittson, Donald Smith, and George Stephen), started from St Paul, and reached Puget Sound, in 1893. This, together with the completion of the Canadian Pacific and the Northern Pacific in 1883, finally opened up the north-west. The completion of the Southern Pacific, from New Orleans across Texas, New Mexico, and Arizona to Southern California, in 1881 had also opened up a new south-west. Mining areas and cattle country that had previously been the haunt of Indians and bison thus became available. During this period several new states were added – Colorado (1876), North Dakota, South Dakota, Washington, and Montana (1889), Wyoming and Idaho (1890).

About 1870, the first shipments of cattle were made from Chicago and became a significant factor. By 1880, refrigerator cars had revolutionized the meat-packing industry, making shipment possible to the East Coast and even to Europe. The slaughtering and packing industries in the United States, worth less than $30 million in 1860, expanded to being worth over $300 million in 1870, and more than $564 million in 1890. In the decade from 1880 to 1890, immigration was again exceptionally high, at somewhere around 5¼ million as opposed to less than 3 million in the previous decade.

Of the immigrants to the United States between 1861 and 1901, a mere 500,000 were Scots. The overall picture of their distribution, however, is clear enough. The greatest numbers were to be found in the mid-Atlantic states, New York, Pennsylvania, and Massachusetts, in that order. Following them in varying degree were the east north-central states (Illinois, Michigan and Ohio) and the Pacific coast states (notably California). States with the most Scottish inhabitants are new York, Pennsylvania, Massachusetts, and Illinois; the cities are New York, Chicago, Philadelphia, and Detroit.

Despite their comparatively small numbers, the Scots made a very considerable impact, as may be seen from a book by G. F. Black, entitled *Scotland's Mark on America*, published in 1921. This lists some 1,500 Scots of importance in the government, armed forces, professions, industry, finance, and the arts. Apart from fifteen judges of the Supreme Court, more than a hundred governors of states since the Revolution are listed, as well as many notable leaders in other fields.

It is worth recording at this point the remarkable parallels between the lives of two notable Scottish academic divines, each of whom made his mark in the United States. The Rev. Dr John Witherspoon (see p. 58) was born a Lowland Scot, graduated at Edinburgh University, and became a minister in the Presbyterian church before going to America in August 1768. He spent the last twenty-six years of his life at Princeton University, where he was President, dying on 15 November 1794. The Rev. Dr Andrew McCosh, also born a Lowland Scot, also graduated at Edinburgh University, becoming a minister in the Presbyterian church before going to America in August 1868. He also spent the last twenty-six years of his life at Princeton, where he too was President, dying on 16 November 1894. Coincidence could scarcely be carried any further.

A Scot who made his name in a different sphere was John Reid, born in Dunfermline in 1840. An ironmaster, he came to the United States in 1866. With another Dunfermline-born friend, Robert Scott Lockhart, he is credited with introducing the game of golf to North America. He laid out a golf-course on his private estate at Yonkers and formed the St Andrew's Golf Club of New York. As well as being its founder and first president, the 'Father of Golf in America', he was also a fine singer of Scots songs, and the 44th President of the St Andrew's Society of New York. He died in 1916.

In 1893, a panic recession spread throughout the United States and confidence did not return for four years. Railway financing had again been desperately reckless and banking methods unsound; these factors combined with an agricultural depression and with financial troubles in the Argentine and Europe. In many ways the resulting recession proved a financial turning-point. After a period of financial chaos, when silver-mining slumped and the farming industry was embittered, companies were concentrated into yet fewer hands. The financier J. Pierpont Morgan came to the rescue of Grover Cleveland in his second term and saved the government in 1894.

In 1897 William McKinley (of Scottish forebears) was elected President after a brilliant campaign by his adviser Marcus Hanna of Ohio (who also had Scottish antecedents). In the decade that followed high finance and combines on a scale never previously conceived, such as Standard Oil, absorbed many weaker competitors. J. Pierpont Morgan, especially, dominated vast areas of business such as transport, coal, mines, and oil. Edward B. Harriman made it his avowed intent to control the entire railroad system. Andrew Carnegie by now was the undisputed steel magnate of Pittsburgh.

Ironmaster, financier, and philanthropist, Andrew Carnegie was also 45th President of the St Andrew's Society of New York, succeeding to John Reid. His term of office ran from 1899 to 1902. After starting the Keystone Bridge Company in 1865, he had never looked back. A brilliant selector of men, he chose many Scots as his colleagues in his mighty Carnegie Steel Company – notably Robert Pitcairn, James Scott, George Lauder, and Charles Lockhart. Retiring at the age of sixty-five in 1902, Carnegie gave away some $333 million in his lifetime, and a further $400 million more was distributed through various agencies he arranged. The St Andrew's Society of New York itself benefited from his generosity to the extent of $200,000. He died in 1919.

Andrew Carnegie, ironmaster, financier and philanthropist – his parents left Glasgow for Pittsburgh in 1848.

In 1901 William McKinley was shot by an anarchist in Buffalo at the start of his second term as President. He was succeeded by Theodore Roosevelt, his Vice-President. By his peacemaking efforts, Roosevelt brought about the termination of the Russo-Japanese War in 1905, at Portsmouth, New Hampshire. By making the Hague tribunal an effective instrument for settling disputes, he gained the approval of Europe as well as America. A dispute with Canada over Alaska was concluded by diplomatic discussion; and an agreement with Panama was ratified in 1907 – a payment and annuity, in return for rights to build an Isthmian Canal. For the first time, America was beginning to play a world role.

In 1904 Roosevelt was triumphantly returned as President. In 1906 the earthquake and fire in San Francisco virtually destroyed the city. In 1908 William Howard Taft followed Roosevelt as President. New states admitted during this period included Oklahoma (1907), and New Mexico and Arizona (1910). In 1912 Woodrow Wilson, whose mother, Jessie Woodrow, was daughter of the Rev. Woodrow of Paisley, became President.

On the outbreak of the First World War in 1914, the United States affirmed its neutrality, and in 1916 Woodrow Wilson was re-elected. In 1917, when the United States finally declared war against Germany, its contribution was considerable. Nearly 4 million were enrolled in the forces; more than 2 million served overseas; 1,300,000 saw active service; 49,000 were killed in action; and 57,000 died of disease, before the war ended on 11 November 1918.

In 1921, Warren G. Hastings became President and on his death in 1923 he was succeeded by Calvin Coolidge who, after serving a second term, was followed by Herbert Hoover in 1929. The Volstead Act, introducing Prohibition, was in force during the years from 1920 to 1932 and proved a nightmare to administer as well as a training-bed for crime. The Ku-Klux-Klan, recreated in the 1920s as a vigilante group, claimed that by 1925 it had a membership of 5 million. It did well in the north and west where it was in part organized by a Scot, David Stephenson of Indiana, who became 'Grand Dragon'. Favourite non-racial targets of the Klansmen were alcohol and adultery, but when Stephenson was convicted for rape the Klan began to decline.

In 1929 came the great slump, when market securities lost an unbelievable $30,000,000,000. In 1932 Franklin Delano Roosevelt was elected President, promptly repealing the Volstead Act and ending Prohibition. In April 1933, the United States left the gold standard; and in 1936 Roosevelt was massively re-elected. The Second World War broke out in Europe in 1939 and once again the United States affirmed its neutrality, agreeing to keep out of the war unless attacked, while giving all possible help to Great Britain. In 1940 Roosevelt accepted a third-term nomination, and was duly re-elected, and the following year the attack on Pearl Harbour shattered the United States' isolation. Forced into the war by this Japanese action, she again allied with Great Britain against Germany. In 1944 Roosevelt was re-elected for an unprecedented fourth term.

By December 1941 there were 1,750,000 US officers and men in the army. In 1942 the US naval forces numbered only 500,000, but by the end of the war they were more than 4 million. By May 1942, 26 million men under the age of forty-five had registered for possible military service, and by the end of the following year there were more than 10 million in the armed forces. In all, 13 million men and women were finally enrolled in the forces. Estimates of the US costs during the war amount to $500,000,000,000. General Douglas Macarthur, of Scots origins, was in charge of the war in the Far East. There, in August 1945, President Harry Truman, who had succeeded on Roosevelt's death earlier in the year, authorized the dropping of the first atomic bombs, which ended the war with Japan's unconditional surrender.

Typical, perhaps, of the many farmers in America who supported the war by growing and rearing as much food as possible, was the Macgregor Land and Livestock Company at Hooper in Washington. Founded originally by four brothers from the Isle of Mull, this 33,000-acre farm raised wheat and sheep. Run during the war by Alexander Campbell Macgregor and his nephew John M. Macgregor, it had 8,000 head of sheep, and grew 40 bushels to the acre of wheat despite an average annual rainfall of only some twelve inches.

In 1948 President Truman was returned for a further four years. Soon afterwards, with high hopes, the United Nations was established as an international body. Then came the Korean War in 1950. Peace was eventually achieved in 1955, but the cost of the United States alone was 35,529 killed in action, and the Cold War still continued. In 1953 General Eisenhower became President, on the general understanding that everyone liked Ike. In 1956 he ran for office again and was re-elected; once more his Vice-President was Richard. M. Nixon.

In 1960 John F. Kennedy became President and in 1961 he

Emigrant Scots have always clung to their traditions: an advertisement for the Scottish Shopper Corporation in America.

took office as a young and glamorous war hero. He was assassinated in 1963 before the euphoria had quite worn off, and was succeeded by Vice-President Lyndon B. Johnson, who was elected President in 1964. The Vietnam War, begun in 1963, dragged on apparently unendingly and even the American successes in space – including the first man on the moon, Neil Armstrong (of Scottish ancestry) – could not compensate for it. President Johnson was succeeded in 1969 by Richard M. Nixon, who at least succeeded in extricating the United States from the morass of Vietnam before the pitiful drama of Watergate was enacted. He was superseded by Vice-President Gerald Ford, who was followed by President Jimmy Carter; and in 1981 he, in turn, was ousted at the polls by President Ronald Reagan.

Throughout its history the United States has owed much to its Scottish emigrants, however small a minority they may have been. The annual emigration of Scots to the United States is indeed probably not much more than around 8,000, but there must be several millions who can proudly claim Scottish forebears on one side or the other. There is also a continual movement of Scots around the world, which makes nonsense of these figures. A typical example is that of the Allardyce family from farming stock near Strathaven in Lanarkshire.

In 1910 the younger son of the Allardyce family, seeing no future in Scottish farming as conditions then were, emigrated to Indiana with his wife and young son, where he farmed successfully. His son, faced with the slump conditions of the 1930s, went to Detroit, where inevitably he was involved with the manufacture of motor cars. His grandson, Randall Allardyce, recalls vividly that every week-end in the 1940s the Scots of the area assembled at a fish-and-chip shop run by a fellow Scot. In the anonymity of a great city he knew at first hand what his relatives, cousins, uncles, and aunts were doing in Strathaven far better than he knew the affairs of his neighbours in Detroit. With a typical emigrant Scot's fervour he learned to play the pipes, and tossed the caber at the Grandfather Mountain Highland Games in North Carolina. When finally qualified as a doctor at Princeton, he returned to Scotland and married a Scots girl; then qualified as a heart specialist in Edinburgh before finally settling in New Zealand.

More common, perhaps, is the movement of emigrant Scots between Canada and the USA, or vice versa. A good example of this may be found in the 69th President of the St Andrew's Society of New York, John Murdoch MacGregor, whose ancestors emigrated from near Lock Katrine to Canada around 1775,

The heads of the sponsoring clans and societies at the 1977 Grandfather Mountain Highland Games, North Carolina.

but who was himself born in North Dakota. The 70th President, Dr Thomas Haig, on the other hand, was born at Kilsyth in the county of Stirling, while the 68th President James A. Keillor was born in Glasgow.

Through such societies emigrant Scots can get together with one another, and it is clear that they enjoy doing so from the quite remarkable proliferation of such societies. There are, for instance, well over fifty St Andrew's Societies in the United States alone, and many of them, like the St Andrew's Society of New York, have a regular news-letter. There are nearer sixty Clan and Family Societies, mostly with their own historians and genealogists. As one example, Mr Charles W. Ferguson of Dallas, a retired oil-insurance executive, genealogist of the Clan Ferguson Society of North America, has researched some four or five hundred pages of family forebears, back to the eighteenth century.

Nor is this by any means all, for there are innumerable pipe-bands throughout the United States. Since as early as 1836 there have also been Highland Societies holding annual Highland Games (such as the Grandfather Mountain Highland Games in N. Carolina, already mentioned) and they too are almost without number. There are, of course, also many Burns Clubs, Highland Dancing Societies, Curling Societies, and other clubs and societies of Scottish interest. There is even a Clans of Hawaii Club. In the United States, the emigrant Scots undoubtedly seem to be strongest in New York, and it was fitting, therefore, that at the first International Clan Gathering held in Edinburgh in 1977 Mayor Lindsay of New York should have led the march past.

Since 1974 there has been set up, under the Presidency of Dr Herbert P. MacNeal of New Jersey, the Council of Scottish Clan Associations, which intends making order out of confusion by bringing these disparate bodies together and exchanging information between them. Through their newsletter, *The Claymore*, and by liaison with other bodies of a similar nature, they may well succeed. It is to be hoped they will, since one of their principal aims is listed as being 'to preserve the customs and traditions of Scotland and to promote appreciation of the Scottish heritage'. That surely sums up the principal motivation of every emigrant Scot.

7

Canada

In 1603 Samuel de Champlain sailed up the St Lawrence and founded the first French colony at Port Royal, now Annapolis, Nova Scotia. In 1608 he founded Quebec. Until his death in 1635 he strove to explore the interior and build up the French colony, although as early as 1613 the settlement at Port Royal was almost wiped out by the English. After his death, however, little was achieved until the formation of a French 'Company of the West Indies' in 1664, by which time the total French population was scarcely more than 2,000. In 1665 a further 2,000 emigrants arrived from France, but not much more was accomplished, and in 1674 the Company's Charter was revoked.

In the 1670s and '80s, Louis, Comte de Frontenac, attacked the Iroquois and kept them under control. He also fought hard against the English, but after Frontenac's death the English pressed home their attacks. By the Treaty of Utrecht in 1713 France acknowledged Britain's claims to Hudson Bay, Newfoundland, and Nova Scotia, but she still retained the shores of the St Lawrence and Cape Breton. In 1744, during the War of the Austrian Succession, the capture of Louisburg was at last effected but at the Peace of Aix-la-Chapelle it was returned to the French. During the Seven Years War beginning in 1756, France lost Quebec to Wolfe in 1759, and in 1760 the French army surrendered at Montreal. By the Peace of Paris in 1763 all of New France, as it was known, was ceded to Great Britain.

During the American War of Independence (1775–1783) many thousands of American Loyalists moved northwards into Canada, to Nova Scotia and what are now Ontario and New Brunswick. These United Empire Loyalists, estimated at around 40,000, introduced a new element into Canadian life, for the original French settlers were now considerably outnumbered by the British. In 1791 the Constitutional Act separated Canada into

Upper and Lower Canada, the former being entirely British and the latter chiefly French.

This was a period of historic exploration. Alexander Mackenzie, born in Stornaway, who had come out to Canada aged sixteen, joined the North West Company in 1787 at the Union of the Companies. Then, at the age of twenty-four, he was appointed to the trading-post on Lake Athabasca, where he built Fort Chipewyan. From there he led an expedition to the Arctic Ocean in 1789. In 1792 he led another expedition to the Pacific Ocean through the Rocky Mountains, travelling within sight of Vancouver Island and returning in 1793 without the loss of a man, after as arduous and dangerous an exploration as any ever accomplished. By his efforts he opened the way to transcontinental travel and trade.

Amongst those who read Alexander Mackenzie's *Journal* was Thomas Douglas, eighth Earl of Selkirk, who had already founded a Scottish settlement on Prince Edward Island in 1803. In the same year 1,000 of the demobilized Glengarry Fencibles went with their families and their chaplain, Alexander Macdonnell, to Glengarry County in Upper Canada, near Montreal. Possibly inspired by this, in 1804 Lord Selkirk tried to form another settlement, composed of United Empire Loyalists, on Lake St Claire; it was named Baldoon after his estate in Scotland. This failed utterly, owing to disease and an extremely bad harvest.

Lord Selkirk, however, remained undiscouraged, and in 1810 he went on to attempt to form another settlement in the Red River area of Hudson Bay, which Mackenzie had mentioned as being very fertile. At this time the Hudson Bay Company and North West Company were each struggling for trade. The North West Company accordingly did their best to sabotage his efforts at settlement, by attacking his settlers and by legal actions. Selkirk himself died in 1820, worn out with the struggle, but the merger of the two companies in 1821 ended the conflict between them and ensured the success of the settlement which he had sited some thirty miles south of Lake Winnipeg, where Winnipeg itself now stands. The choice of first governor to unite the companies fell on another Scot, George Simpson, later knighted for his success in that task and in opening up vast areas of new land during his long period of rule.

In 1812, war was declared between Britain and the United

States of America because of commercial disagreements and the unwarranted treatment of United States shipping by British warships. The United States saw this as an opportunity to annex Canada, but the Canadians disliked republicanism and refused to support them. There was considerable action around Niagara, however, until peace was achieved by the Treaty of Ghent in 1814. Thereafter, despite one or two awkward incidents, peace was maintained, and in 1817 Lord Castlereagh and President Monroe agreed on the disarming of the Canadian and United States border. The following year, in 1818, they also agreed on the definition of the border, so that what had previously promised to lead to further hostilities was amicably settled.

In the 1820s there was a good deal of canal-building, and in 1825 the Great Erie Canal was completed. Within four years, the Welland Canal bypassing Niagara and joining Lakes Ontario and Erie was also constructed by the enterprising John Hamilton Merritt. In 1826 Alexander Galt, the Scottish novelist, went out to Canada as secretary of the Canadian Land Company. He opened up a road through thick forest between Lakes Huron and Erie, and also founded the town of Guelph. He was misrepresented to his directors by the governing clique, known as the Family Compact, and left Canada in 1829. His son, Alexander Tulloch Galt, emigrated to Canada in 1835 as secretary of the British-American Land Company, and later entered Canadian politics, playing no mean part.

The so-called Family Compact was a considerable check on Canadian advancement at times. Robert Gourlay, who left Scotland for Canada in 1817 and set up as a land agent, made powerful enemies while attempting to stimulate further emigration. Subjected to the same sort of 'Upper Canada Justice' which Lord Selkirk had found hard to combat, he was gaoled on perjured evidence before a corrupt Chief Justice. Although he tried to take out a writ of habeas corpus, he remained in gaol for seven months without trial before being deported to the United States. It was not until 1841 that his arrest and sentence were publicly condemned by the Canadian Parliament.

Another Scot, William Lyon Mackenzie, attacked the corruption of the Compact. He founded a newspaper, the *Colonial Advocate*, and in 1828 was elected a member of the Assembly for York county. In 1831 he was expelled for libelling the Assembly in his columns. In the next three years, like a Canadian Wilkes, he was expelled and re-elected four times. In 1835 he was elected first Mayor of Toronto and in the same year his party of reform triumphed in the Assembly. He was then appointed Chairman of a committee enquiring into 'grievances'.

A new Governor, F. B. Head, sent out by Lord Glenelg, the bumbling Colonial Secretary, backed the Compact against Mackenzie. The Compact triumphed at the next election and Mackenzie lost his seat. The fiery little Scotsman was clearly veering towards republicanism, and by 1835 was not far from open rebellion. In the circumstances, considering the corrupt state of the governing clique, this was not altogether surprising.

In Lower Canada a very similar state of affairs existed, for there a French Canadian, Louis-Joseph Papineau, was the leader of a reforming group. In 1834 he advocated democracy in both church and state and by May of 1837, like Mackenzie, he was on the verge of open rebellion. The effect of a severe economic slump in the months that followed, owing to a recession in the United States, to crop failures throughout Canada, and to a decrease in trade with Britain, brought many small farmers to the brink of ruin and desperation. The time was ripe for rebellion.

Following a riot in Montreal, Papineau withdrew to the country, thinking that his presence might inflame matters. The government mistook this as an attempt to raise armed followers. Arrests followed, and there were numerous clashes. Papineau and his principal aides fled to the safety of the United States. Meanwhile in Upper Canada, Mackenzie took the news of the clashes in Lower Canada as a signal for a general uprising. He issued a stirring call to action, but after meeting at Montgomery's Tavern, four miles north of Toronto, his motley collection of followers promptly dispersed when the first troops arrived on the scene. Mackenzie himself followed Papineau's example and withdrew in haste to the United States.

Although both these revolts were entirely ineffectual, the fact that they occurred at the time of Queen Victoria's accession to the throne drew considerable attention to them. In 1838 the Earl of Durham was sent out as Governor and was requested to submit a report on affairs in Canada. He only spent some five months there, however, since his leniency towards the leaders of the revolts was strongly criticized at home and he promptly resigned.

Despite his short stay, his report, which was published in 1839, was a masterly summing-up of Canadian affairs. He recommended the Union of the two Canadian provinces and the ultimate union of all British North America, with the granting of self-government to the resulting state. Accordingly in 1840 the Act of Union was passed, uniting the Provinces of Upper and Lower Canada.

The first Governor sent out in 1840 was Charles Poulett Thompson, Baron Sydenham and Toronto. By this time there were more than a million people in Canada and its importance was rapidly growing. In the single Parliament both provinces were equally represented, but inevitably each was suspicious and jealous of the other, which resulted in frequent deadlocks. Lord Sydenham died in 1841, before he had time to effect much in the way of change.

Whether as explorers, settlers, governors, or soap-box orators and agitators, Scots were prominent throughout the growth of Canada in every sphere open to them. Their attitudes are perhaps best reflected in their letters, such as those written by David Maclaren in the 1840s from Torbolton in Canada to his brother in Perthshire.

David Maclaren had moved from Perthshire to the Trongate of Glasgow for three or four years after his marriage. There he had a share in a drysalters, or ironmongers. After four years he set off for Canada with his wife and two sons. In 1821, after a few months in Ottawa, they moved to Richmond and thence to Torbolton, where he established a small sawmill and farm, and where he lived until his sons were grown up. In a letter headed Torbolton, 12 December 1840, he wrote to his brother in Perthshire as follows:

Yours of the 15th July reached this on the 26th of August – much sooner than letters from your quarters used to do . . . James is 22 years of age, John, 20, David 18, Henry 16, William 12, Alexander 8. The three eldest, with a hired Hewer and occasionally an additional hand, have commenced the winter operation of making timber, a business we shall probably close this season as it interferes I find somewhat with farming operations, particularly with clearing land . . . The two next boys does partly the threshing – attends to the cattle and chops the firewood. Alexander the youngest I must set down as doing nothing. I may say that none of them have ever been at school. There has been none within our reach and the deficiency has had to be supplied in the best way we could by my tuition. James has gone very successfully through common and decimal Arithmetic and Trigonometry, knows a little Geometry and Geography – none of the others are as far advanced as James, they have all, however, a tolerable share of natural abilities and want only time for study and a good teacher to make them passable scholars. Of the three youngest, William seems the fondest of learning and should any favourable opportunity occur I mean to push him forward in the way he inclines . . . I too have been adding to my little pendicle, which previously consisted of 400 Acres. The addition however is more than four times the original . . .'

In April 1842, by which time the Canada Act of 1840 with its provisions for self-government had begun to take effect, David Maclaren wrote again to his brother:

. . . I thank you for the kind offer of a home for one of my boys in the event of my sending him over to school. I may perhaps yet avail myself of your good offer, but I am for the present inclined to wait until I shall see the result of our new School Act . . . I am sorry to perceive that the distress of manufacturing districts is still very great. What effect will this have on emigration? From the great efforts of late making on both sides of the Atlantic it is I believe to be expected that the tide of emigration will flow very strong to Canada this season . . . If any of your neighbours take the notion of emigrating you may on my knowledge of the country safely recommend them Ottawa from Bytown upwards . . . In regard to our new house, should you feel any curiosity about the construction of such a wooden tenement, I shall perhaps send you a 'full and particular account' . . .

The Maclarens were well settled, as these letters indicate, and went on to found a dynasty. They were not, like many frontier settlers, continually on the move. From the arrival of the United Empire Loyalists, there was a quite distinct spearhead of settlers constantly opening up new ground. This was in itself a skilled task

In this sketch of the interior of a log cabin at the Red River settlement, Canada, a Scotsman can be seen, wearing a tam o' shanter and seated right.

requiring particular knowledge and skills which were only acquired by experience.

The ability to clear ground with an axe, to make a log cabin, furniture and farmsteading, was a prerequisite of the frontier settler. The wife had to be able to weave, spin, knit, make soap, and know the useful wild herbs and fruits, as well as having a knowledge of medicine and farming and being able to cook in primitive conditions, while withstanding the isolation and drudgery. When the land was cleared, it was notable that these frontiersmen began to feel dissatisfied and wished to move on, just as the first emigrants came out to buy new farms. There were, inevitably, many Scots amongst these pioneers, as well as amongst the politicians and provincial rulers.

It was a Scot, as Governor, who was the first to establish the worth of the new constitution. James Bruce, eighth Earl of Elgin, was appointed Governor of Canada in 1847. When the Rebellion Losses Bill was passed by a large majority, intended to compensate any who had suffered losses in the rebellion of 1837, it was easily misrepresented as being a proposal to compensate rebels.

The Governor was bombarded with petitions against the bill, but held strongly to the principle that he should not interfere with decisions passed by the Canadian Parliament affecting domestic matters. He gave the bill the Royal Assent, thus making responsible government in Canada a reality at last.

There was an immediate storm of protest and the mob rose and rioted in Montreal. Lord Elgin's carriage was hooted, hissed, and pelted with rotten eggs and stones. Parliament House, with the valuable records it contained, was burned down. But Lord Elgin remained firmly impervious to public opinion and in due course it was appreciated that he had acted both wisely and well. The fact that the measure favoured the French minority made him particularly popular with them, but the major point was that it was the first step towards independent rule for Canada.

It was not because of dissatisfaction at the way things were going in Canada, but more probably simply because of a very bad season's harvest in Cape Breton and an enthusiastic report on Australia from one of his sons, that the Rev. Norman MacLeod decided in 1850 to emigrate with his flock. This extraordinary spell-binding divine, who preached his own brand of 'Normanism', or rigid Calvinism, had left Loch Broom in 1817 for Pictou in Nova Scotia and had persuaded 150 of his followers to join him in 1818. In 1820 he then led the members of his sect on to St Ann's in Cape Breton, where in 1821 others joined them from both Pictou and Scotland. There he became official magistrate in 1823. Although already both leader and preacher, he was only finally ordained in 1827 by a presbytery of the State of New York. His rule, insisting on extreme observance of the Sabbath, amounted to a tyranny.

In 1851 the first shipload of 140 Normanists left St Ann's for Adelaide, before moving on to Melbourne. Both were pronounced unsatisfactory, and a second shipload arriving in 1852 found no settlement awaiting them. Norman MacLeod then decided to try New Zealand, and eventually a small settlement was formed on the Waipu River in North Island. From there they sent word to the remaining St Ann's settlers, and between 1855 and 1860 another four shiploads duly sailed for New Zealand. Although protracted movements were not uncommon for Scots emigrants before finally settling, this seemed to be carrying things rather far by any standards.

In 1854 at the end of his term as Governor, Lord Elgin negotiated a reciprocity Treaty with the United States of America which gave Canadian farm-products free entry to the American market. The outbreak of the American Civil War in 1861 resulted in increased demand in the United States, and Canada found a booming market for the whole of the war. In 1865, however, with the end of the war and of the first ten years of the Treaty, it was not renewed – on the grounds, amongst others, that it was a one-sided bargain.

In 1849 the Colony of Vancouver Island was created, primarily to prevent the Americans from claiming it by default. Initially, however, like the prairies, this part of the Pacific Coast was managed by the Hudson Bay Company. In 1856, when the Cariboo gold strike was bringing prospectors north, the Governor (a Scot named James Douglas) simply proclaimed his authority over the mainland. He was fortunately backed by the government in Britain, and in 1858 the Colony of British Columbia was duly established.

From 1854 the combination of John A. Macdonald (a young lawyer from Kingston, Ontario, who had been born in Glasgow in 1815) and Georges Etienne Cartier (a French-Canadian lawyer), dominated the Canadian political scene for many years, especially during the important period of Confederation. With the aid of George Brown (Scottish-born editor of the Toronto *Globe*, who wielded great influence in Western Canada) and of Alexander T. Galt (son of the Scottish novelist, who had the ear of the business community in the East) they managed to push this all-important legislation through effectively. It was thus a largely Scottish initiative that achieved a united Canada at last.

When the Maritime states – New Brunswick, Nova Scotia, and Prince Edward Island – were considering federation in 1864, it was Macdonald who proposed a broader plan to include Canada as well. In October a conference was held behind closed doors in Quebec. The principal Canadian negotiators were Macdonald, Cartier, Brown, and Galt. The plan for federation outlined by the Quebec Conference was almost entirely Macdonald's. With slight modifications it was passed, as the British North America Act, in 1867 and the Dominion of Canada was thus established. In recognition of his services to the Empire, John A. Macdonald was made a KCB, and it was as Sir John A. Macdonald that he became the first premier of the dominion.

In 1869 the North-West Territories were secured as part of Canada by purchase of the rights of the Hudson Bay Company, and the Hon. W. McDougall was appointed first Governor. The mainly half-breed population of the Red River area, however, resented the transfer of control, about which they had not been consulted. Disaffection was fomented by United States immigrants hoping for annexation, and a fanatical half-breed named Louis Riel led a rebellion, establishing what was termed a 'provisional government' which prevented McDougall from entering the territory. A white settler, Thomas Scott, who resisted the rebels was shot in 1870 at Fort Garry, and the act aroused intense indignation. An armed force of British regulars and Canadian volunteers marched to Fort Garry, but the rebels had scattered and Riel had fled. Meanwhile an Act had been passed creating Manitoba a province and in due course Fort Garry was renamed Winnipeg, the doorway to the Western prairies.

In 1871 British Columbia also joined the Confederation, on the promise that the Canadian Pacific Railway link between east and west coasts would be built within ten years; a promise that the Liberal opposition, led by another Scots Canadian, Alexander Mackenzie, claimed it was impossible to fulfill. In 1873 Prince Edward Island, which had refused to join the Confederation in 1864, was persuaded to do so on a promise of 'more favourable terms'.

In 1872 two companies were formed and received charters to built the Canadian Pacific Railway, with a Scots-Canadian at the head of each company. The Hon. David Macpherson of Toronto was president of one and Sir Hugh Allan of Montreal of the other. The government tried to bring about an amalgamation of the two companies, on the grounds that it was a national undertaking which required the concentrated resources of a single company, but before they had succeeded the general election of 1872 took place, at which Sir John A. Macdonald's party was returned, although with a reduced majority.

Following the election, charges of corruption were made against Sir John A. Macdonald, alleging that he had taken money from Sir Hugh Allan to support his party. He rejected the charges, but resigned. When the Liberal leader, Mr Alexander

Sergeants of the 78th Highlanders, Canada, 1867.

Mackenzie, went to the country he was elected by an overwhelming majority. An ex-stonemason, the most damning comment made of him was that he was 'a stonemason still'. Though cautious to a fault, nevertheless his administration continued in power for five years. Meanwhile with a greatly diminished following, but gallant in defeat, Sir John A. Macdonald continued to act as leader of the opposition.

It is interesting to note that during the 1860s and '70s two Highland units were raised in Canada, both in Nova Scotia. The first was the 79th Highland Battalion of Infantry, later known as the Pictou Highlanders and ultimately as the 1st Battalion Nova Scotia Highlanders. The other was the 94th Highland Provisional Battalion of Infantry, later known as the Cape Breton Highlanders, and ultimately as the 2nd Battalion Nova Scotia Highlanders. From this stage onwards, Scottish influence in the Canadian army was to grow more marked.

Throughout the nineteenth century the Scottish influence on education in Canada was particularly notable. Many settlers, like David Maclaren, were capable after an ordinary Scottish schooling of educating their sons to a high standard, imparting a working knowledge of decimal arithmetic and trigonometry. Interest in learning was universal amongst the Scots settlers, even though some may have been less competent than David Maclaren. Many of the isolated settlements brought their own teachers with them, or else relied on the minister, whether Catholic or Presbyterian, to make good this deficiency – usually with success.

The Presbyterian influence on Canadian higher education, was also considerable. Notable Presbyterian colleges were founded, such as Moorin College in Quebec City, Pictou Academy in Nova Scotia, Queen's College in Kingston, and Manitoba College in Winnipeg, as well as Dalhousie College in New Brunswick. Scottish influence through principals and administrators, was apparent in McGill, Trinity College, and the Universities of New Brunswick and Toronto. It should also be noted that the St Francis Xavier University of Nova Scotia was originated by Catholic Highlanders and there are still some among the staff whose first language was once Gaelic. One of the principal reasons for this bias towards Scottish educationists was simply that Scottish graduates could be obtained at much less than the cost of Oxford or Cambridge graduates, while their standards were quite as high.

In Canadian literature, as elsewhere throughout the world, the Scots produced poets and writers, though the latter often turned to journalism. Perhaps the best known of Scottish poets in the period before the Confederation was Alexander McLauchlan, who emigrated from Glasgow in 1840. Inspired by Burns, he chose similar targets for satire (such as the 'unco' guid') as well as some specifically Canadian ones. In one of his better known poems, 'We Live in a Rickety House', he attacked the Bible-punchers sardonically:

Ye clog the soil of nature
With your wretched little creeds,
Then hold up your hands in wonder
At the dearth of noble deeds.

He also satirized the money-conscious attitudes of many of the
duller settlers he saw around him:

Talk not of old cathedral woods,
Their gothic arches throwing,
John only sees in all those trees
So many saw-logs growing.
He laughs at all our ecstasies
And he keeps still repeating,
'You say 'tis fair, but will it wear?
And is it good for eating?'

He published three books of poetry, his last, *Songs and Poems*, in
1874 during the massive recession which persisted throughout
Mackenzie's administration from 1872–77. During that time the
United States refused to consider any suggestions for improving
trade between the two countries. Accordingly Sir John A. Macdonald proposed a system of tariff protection for Canadian industry.

The Liberals, meanwhile, still clung to their outmoded policy
of Free Trade. Furthermore they had withdrawn the promise to
build the Canadian Pacific Railway link within ten years on the
grounds that it was impossible of fulfilment, with resulting
ill-feeling in British Columbia and talk of secession. The net
result was that at the next election in 1875 Sir John A. Macdonald
was returned to power once more with a considerable majority,
and his premiership continued without further breaks until his
death in 1891, while his party remained in power until 1896.

Sir John A. Macdonald's bold policies for rapid development
appealed to a growing and ambitious country far more than
Mackenzie's cautious measures. Immediately on regaining power
he introduced his system of tariff protection, and followed it by a
contract with a new company to build the transcontinental rail link
within ten years. The terms were exceptionally high, and required
vigorous debate before being passed in 1881; they included a
grant of $25 million and 25 million acres of land. Even so, the

company was forced to obtain a government loan of a further $20 million secured against their land, which was repaid in 1887.

The railway was opened in November 1886, five years before schedule, by Mr Donald A. Smith, later Lord Strathcona, one of its more notable Scots Canadian backers. There was a strong Scottish element amongst the other prominent Canadian business men involved. They included Mr Duncan McIntyre, Mr R. B. Angus and Mr George Stephen, later Lord Mountstephen, who had been born in Dufftown in 1829, the son of a carpenter.

Before the completion of the Canadian Pacific Railway there was another uprising in the North-West Territories. Petitions pointing to the various causes of distress in the area had been ignored by the government in the east, and, as with the Red River rising in 1870, and for many of the same reasons, a degree of self-government was felt to be essential. Louis Riel, who had emigrated to Montana to avoid trial for treason and who was now a schoolmaster, was called on to return and lead another 'provisional government'.

The rebellion this time took on serious dimensions, for it was accompanied by an Indian uprising and the massacre of the village of Frog Lake. Seven thousand militia were sent by the CPR to Saskatchewan, arriving there with speed and thus vindicating the building of the railway before it was even completed. Two sharp engagements soon dispersed the rebels, and Riel surrendered. Although clearly insane, he refused to plead insanity and he, along with several Indian chiefs who had been concerned in the massacre, was executed in November 1885.

In the 1891 election Sir John A. Macdonald's protectionist policy proved triumphant once more, and his party was returned to power yet again. Soon after the election, however, Sir John died. His successors were short-lived, and in 1896 the Liberals once more came to power, although forced to maintain the protectionist policies they had so long opposed.

In 1896 gold was discovered in the Yukon, and the gold rush was soon under way in an area best remembered by the verse of Robert Service. Although born in Lancashire Robert Service was brought up in Glasgow before emigrating to Canada. He created the epic heroes Dan McGrew and Sam McGee, as typical of the Yukon country. A good example of his verse is:

This is the Law of the Yukon, that only the Strong shall thrive;
That surely the Weak shall perish, and only the Fit survive.

The declaration of war with the Boers in South Africa in 1899
provided an opportunity to demonstrate Canadian loyalty to
Britain, and the High Commissioner for Canada in London,
Lord Strathcona, raised and equipped a regiment of Canadian
horse, known appropriately as Lord Strathcona's Horse, entirely
at his own expense. Three separate contingents of volunteers
were despatched to South Africa in the course of the war. On the
face of it, Canada was demonstrating her support for the Empire
under the French-Canadian Premier Sir Wilfred Laurier, whose
slight French accent contrasted with the Scottish accent which
Sir John A. Macdonald had never lost. Nevertheless, the Canadians maintained their own independence in the face of the first
cracks in the imperial façade.

Prior to the outbreak of the First World War in 1914, there was
the apparent threat of a depression in Canada. With the outbreak
of the war it was soon forgotten. Under the premiership of Robert
Laird Borden, yet another Canadian Scot, Canada entered the
war wholeheartedly on the British side. Strangely enough, the
Department of Militia and Defence ignored the militia which
existed and enlisted troops instead in a series of numbered
Canadian Expeditionary Force Battalions, several of which were
given Scottish titles. The 13th Battalion was named the Royal
Highlanders of Canada, the 15th became the 48th Highlanders of
Canada, and the 16th the Canadian Scottish. Also among Cana-
dian-Scottish regiments serving in the Canadian Expeditionary
Force, both officers and men wearing the kilt, were the Cameron
Highlanders of Canada, the Seaforth Highlanders of Canada,
and the Nova Scotia Highlanders.

With these, and many other battalions, the Canadian Army
Corps amounted eventually to four divisions of some 600,000
men. In addition, more then 8,000 men enlisted in the navy,
standing guard on the Atlantic approaches, and another 24,000
entered the air force. By 1918 more than 60,000 Canadians had
been killed in action.

During the war, however, the economy boomed. Exports of all
sorts from Canada rose dramatically: wood, lumber, meat, livestock, and metals all reached unimagined export levels, while those

of grain and flour more than doubled in value. The U-Boat blockade of Britain had little effect on Canada's prosperity.

After the war came the reckoning, with the strikes of 1919 which paralysed the nation and effectively proved the power of the unions. The Winnipeg general strike lasted for six weeks until the federal government had the leaders arrested. With the promise of a royal commission of investigation, and with their leaders in gaol, the strike committees then agreed to end the deadlock.

In the 1921 election William Lyon Mackenzie King, grandson of William Lyon Mackenzie, became Premier. An amazingly astute politician, Mackenzie King was to set a record for longevity as Prime Minister. He was returned to office with remarkable regularity and retired finally only in 1948.

With the mid-1920s boom, he was re-elected in 1925 as a minority government, and by sharp political practice he wrong-footed both the Governor General, Lord Byng, and his political opponents by provoking a constitutional crisis. Faced with defeat in the house, he asked Lord Byng to dissolve Parliament, but Byng perfectly correctly refused to do so, and requested his political opponent Meighen to form a government. However, Meighen too found himself unable to form a government, and Lord Byng was forced to dissolve Parliament after all. Mackenzie King then appealed to the electorate on the entirely false argument that Lord Byng had in some way infringed 'Canadian autonomy', winning the ensuing election by blatant appeals for Canadian freedom from imperial interference.

In the 1923 Imperial Conference, the dominions acquired the right to negotiate their own treaties and pursue their own foreign policies, subject to the courtesy of multi-lateral exchange of information. In 1931 came the Statute of Westminster, which gave complete autonomy to the dominions. Thus was the Empire-Commonwealth restructured in the 1920s and '30s.

The 1929 New York stockmarket collapse resulted in ruin for hundreds of thousands of Canadians. During the 1930s, Canada's gross national product and national income declined. In the prairies and the Maritime provinces there was financial and social collapse, with fishermen and farmers left destitute. Unable to produce any panacea, Mackenzie King was resoundingly defeated in the 1930 election, but in 1935, turning the tables on his opponents, he was once again in power.

William Lyon Mackenzie King, Prime Minister of Canada over much of the period 1921–1948; and grandson of William Lyon Mackenzie, a prominent Scottish-Canadian politician of the 1830s.

During this period, from 1935 to 1940 when he died, Lord Tweedsmuir, perhaps more widely known as John Buchan the author, served as Governor-General. Scots-born and retiring, he nevertheless proved immensely popular throughout Canada. With a sound background knowledge of Canadian history and dominion protocol, he proved a useful guide to politicians on both sides of the house.

Canadian links with Scotland between the wars were maintained in many ways, although during the long years of recession emigration slowed almost to a halt. Yet strangely enough there was a strong swing amongst the militia units towards renaming the old Canadian numbered regiments with Scottish titles, and adopting the kilt and pipes. In 1920, the 50th and 88th amalgamated to become the Canadian Scottish. In 1922, the 43rd became the Ottawa Highlanders, and in 1933 it was renamed the Cameron Highlanders of Canada. In 1924, the 103rd became the Calgary Highlanders; in 1927, the 21st became the Essex Scottish, the 42nd became the Lanark and Renfrew Scottish, and the 59th became the Stormont, Dundas, and Glengarry Highlanders. All wore the kilt, but in 1931 the 20th became the Lorne Rifles (in 1936 to be renamed the Lorne Scots) proudly wearing the trews.

With the outbreak of war in 1939, Mackenzie King was still firmly in control as Prime Minister. His somewhat naive and ineffectual approaches to Adolf Hitler before Munich and the outbreak of war, indicated that international politics was certainly not his metier, but to be fair he never pretended that it was. He was always essentially a Canadian for Canada. Nevertheless, with the declaration of war in 1939 he never hesitated for a moment about aligning Canada firmly alongside Britain, and in yet another election in 1940 he once again emerged the victor.

Canada's participation in the Second World War was even greater and more wholehearted than it had been during the First. It was as an arsenal and long-range base for Britain that Canada played her primary role. A Canadian army consisting of three infantry divisions, two armoured divisions, and a further two tank brigades, was sent overseas, with many Scottish regiments included amongst them. There were airfields, maintenance bases and training units across Canada, in which thousands of air-crews from Britain and the Commonwealth were trained. Forty-five squadrons of the Royal Canadian Air Force fought overseas. The Royal Canadian Navy expanded amazingly – from 5,000 to more than 100,000 ships, varying from corvettes to destroyers – and took part in Atlantic convoys as far as Murmansk. It was scarcely surprising that 42,000 Canadians were killed in action, and even that is no final measure of her enormous contribution to the outcome of the war.

In 1948 Mackenzie King retired, after twenty-one years in

office, and was succeeded by Louis St Laurent, who remained in office until 1957. The end of Mackenzie King's long premiership was fittingly marked, after lengthy negotiations which he had initiated, by Newfoundland's agreement in 1949 to join the Confederation as its tenth province. The general standard of living there was below that of the Canadian Maritime provinces, and the prospect of sharing in Canadian prosperity and social welfare programmes encouraged the decision.

Through the Diefenbaker, Pearson, and Trudeau govern-ments in the 1960s and '70s, through the Cold War and the many political and social upsets throughout the world, Canada has continued to prosper. As only one example, the descendants of David Maclaren are still flourishing. His eldest son, James, founded the James Maclaren Company Ltd, an extensive lumber company with mills in Buckingham on the Lievre River. In due course he became President of the Bank of Ottawa (no mean tribute to his father's arithmetic lessons); and after his death the Company continued to be run successfully by his family, expand-ing into hydropower. It is still directed by his descendants, who include six grandsons and three great-grandsons. There is an annual family gathering of more than seventy members, now distinguished in many fields of endeavour.

Interest in family genealogy, as is the case in the United States, is very considerable. The work of Dr E. D. MacPhee, Emeritus Dean of the University of British Columbia, *The Mythology, Traditions and History of MacDhubhsith-MacDuffie Clan* in seven volumes, would appeal to any Scot. Frank Darroch's *A Darroch Family in Scotland and Canada*, tracing some 1,200 descendants of his great-grandfather and the history of the Darrochs from Toronto back to the sixteenth century, is also a work of great interest. Such feats as that of Mr William H. MacEwen, who tracked his ancestors back to 1790 when his great-great-great-grandfather was granted land at Merigonish, Pictou County, Nova Scotia, (when the 82nd Regiment, or Duke of Hamilton's, was returning home) are by no means unusual.

Throughout Canada, as in the United States, there are Scot-tish Societies, St Andrew's Societies, Clan Societies, Burns Clubs, country dancing societies, pipe-bands, Highland Games societies, and many others. Their profusion alone indicates the vast interest in Scottish matters. Of particular interest, however, is the comparatively recently formed Fraoch Eilean Canadian Foundation, a non-profit-making government-sponsored foundation for the purpose of contributing to 'schemes and undertakings . . . for . . . fostering and/or preserving Canadian and Scottish history and culture, *in Canada and elsewhere* . . . to assist in research and publication of Scottish history and culture . . .'

An attempt is being made to keep these societies in touch with each other by the Clans and Scottish Societies in Canada (Cassoc) formed in 1975 and facing a major task of organization under its President Donald C. R. Campbell. There is also a bi-monthly magazine *The Clansman*, produced in Ontario and sold all round the world, specifically aimed at the interests of overseas Scots. All these indicate the enormous interest amongst Canadians in their Scottish heritage.

It must be remembered, of course, that the Gaelic language remained the principal tongue of many communities, especially in Cape Breton and Nova Scotia, until well into this century. Both the Presbyterian faith and Roman Catholicism flourished in communities where only Gaelic was spoken by the early settlers, although subsequently these became bi-lingual. Gaelic newspapers were still circulating as late as the 1930s, and some attempt to revive them has recently been made.

The very place-names of countless areas in Canada reveal the Scottish background of those who named them, even if these settlers have long since moved elsewhere; for example Fort Mackenzie, Fort Grahame, Mount Forbes, the Bruce Mines and Campbellford, to take only a few at random. There are eleven counties in Ontario with Scottish names, and local place-names are found almost everywhere, to a greater or lesser degree. It is also possible to relate Canadian interest in curling and golf to Scottish origins.

As the third largest ethnic group in. Canada, it is scarcely surprising that the Scots have made their mark so strongly. When a leading French-Canadian Cabinet Minister in the government of Quebec is named Robert Burns, it is indicative that the 2,000,000 acknowledged Canadians of Scottish origins have somewhat stronger roots in the nation than might appear just on the strength of mere statistics. The immigration figures since the Second World War speak for themselves: 9,201 Scottish emigrants arrived in Canada in 1951 as opposed to 19,109 English (though there is no indication as to how many of those English, if asked, would themselves have claimed Scottish origins): in 1956 the figures were 10,939 to 32,389; while in 1957 they were 23,514 to 72,476. The proportion of Scots to English emigrants bears no relation to the relative populations of the two countries, some five million as against forty million. Scots have continued to emigrate to Canada at a far higher rate than the English, and many Scots in Scotland feel their ties with Canada are closer than with any other Commonwealth country.

8

Australia

It was perhaps an example of the lack of regard by then accorded to Scotland that David Collins's volumes of 1789–1802 should have been entitled *An Account of the English Colony in New South Wales*. Inevitably there had been a number of Scots amongst the first fleet pioneers, the name given to those sailing with the first convict fleet to Botany Bay which had arrived in New South Wales in 1787. Outstanding amongst them was Captain John Hunter. When it had been decided to found the Colony in 1786, Captain Arthur Phillip had been appointed Commander of the fleet and Governor of the Colony, with Captain John Hunter, in command of HMS *Sirius*, as second-in-command with a dormant commission to act as Governor in the event of Captain Arthur Phillip's absence or death.

There were also, no doubt, some Scots amongst the convicts transported in the first fleet in 1787, as there were thereafter in the regular fleets arriving each year until transportation to New South Wales and Van Diemen's Land (later renamed Tasmania) was ended in 1840. It was begun again a few years later to Western Australia, at that time known as the Swan River Colony, and continued there until as late as 1868, but the proportion of Scots was not large, although exact figures are unknown.

Amongst the earliest convicts transported from Scotland were the political reformers known as the Scottish Martyrs, although not all were Scottish. A Scottish Convention of the Friends of the People had been called in Edinburgh in December 1792, at a time of general fear of revolution; the Lord Advocate, Robert Dundas, undoubtedly over-reacted to news of correspondence with the revolutionary French and the meeting of liberal-minded reform societies. Thomas Muir, an advocate and the Vice-President, William Skirving, the secretary, Joseph Gerrald and Maurice Margarot, delegates from England, were all sentenced to fourteen years' transportation for sedition, and Thomas Palmer a clergyman was sentenced to seven.

They were transported in 1794, but were treated with special consideration, being free from restraint within the bounds of the colony. Muir and Skirving both bought small farms and Palmer engaged in several small commercial undertakings. Muir was the only one to effect his escape in 1796, but died in Paris in 1799. Gerrald and Skirving both died in New South Wales within a month or so of Muir's escape. Palmer served his time, and later died on the island of Guam. Margarot, after making himself a nuisance to successive governors, returned to England in 1810 and died in poverty in 1815.

In the days when stealing a handkerchief was a capital offence, transportation must have seemed lenient enough. Nowadays, of course, it is doubtful if many of the delinquents transported would even come to trial: it is unlikely that many were criminals in the real sense of the word. Most of those transported were probably driven to petty theft by sheer hunger in the harsh economic conditions caused by the industrial revolution.

From the earliest days there seem to have been a number of Scots amongst the administrators and some amongst the free settlers both in New South Wales and Van Diemen's Land, although in nothing like the numbers in which they were to come during the first half of the nineteenth century. Captain John Macarthur, born in England of Argyllshire parents, who went out to New South Wales as an Army officer in 1790, was not untypical, although a more forceful character than most. There is little doubt that he was instrumental in causing Governor John Hunter to be recalled in 1800.

In 1795 Macarthur acquired some farmland and started breeding sheep. In 1796 he was the first to introduce merino sheep on which the Australian economy was to be based during much of the century which followed. Both he and his four sons, Edward, John, James, and William, were to exercise considerable influence in the political as well as agricultural spheres, throughout that entire period.

The Scots certainly made their mark in Australia in the nineteenth century. Of the first six governors of New South Wales, three were Scots. John Hunter was born in Leith – the only East Coast man amongst them, for Lachlan Macquarie came from Ulva, an island west of Mull in Argyll, and his successor Sir Thomas Brisbane came from Largs on the Ayrshire coast.

John Hunter was an able, courageous, and conscientious Governor, but on taking office he found a virtually impossible situation. The military had assumed control of the civil administration, including the courts, management of lands, public stores, and convict labour. The officers concerned had also developed a tremendous traffic in spirits, from which they made great profits. Hunter determined to return all these powers to the civil administration, but was fiercely opposed, particularly by John Macarthur. Anonymous letters were sent to London, accusing Hunter of the very abuses he was trying to control. In the circumstances there was little he could do.

Captain John Macarthur, of Argyllshire stock, who introduced into Australia in 1796 the merino sheep, on which the country's economy was to be based during much of the following century.

His great interest was in natural science, and he promoted expeditions procuring specimens of the lyrebird, the koala, the platypus, and the wombat. David Collins's account of the platypus, 'an amphibious animal of the mole kind', was undoubtedly written by Hunter. On his recall to London he wrote a pamphlet convincingly refuting the charges of financial maladministration made against him. He soon became recognized as an authority on the Colony and most of his suggested reforms were eventually implemented.

In 1805 William Bligh, of *Bounty* notoriety, was appointed Governor, but due to his harshness and maladministration he was deposed in 1808 by a forthright Scot, Major George Johnston of the 102nd Foot, and was imprisoned until 1809; when another Scot, William Paterson, was appointed interim administrator and expelled both Bligh and Johnston, sending them back to England to stand their trials.

In the meantime, in 1809 in England it was decided to send out General Nightingall as Governor and General Lachlan Macquarie as Lieutenant-Governor in command of the 73rd Highlanders, the 2nd Battalion of the Black Watch – the only kilted Scottish regiment sent out to Australia in the nineteenth century. Before even setting out, however, Nightingall resigned because of ill-health, and Macquarie was gazetted Governor in his place. He found the Colony 'barely emerging from an infantile imbecility'. He reorganized the public administration and ended the 'rum traffic', a system of payment by spirits; he also maintained a public works programme, providing decent public buildings for the principal towns such as Sydney, Hobart, and Newcastle.

Although he intended to stay only three or four years, his lengthy term in office was only once exceeded, and that in the twentieth century. He encouraged exploration, so that in 1813 the Blue Mountains were crossed and the Australian interior was opened up for the first time. He also initiated ambitious road-building schemes, encouraged education and literature, and provided a public library. He even appointed Massey Robinson as Poet Laureate, with an annual salary of two cows. His policy towards time-expired convicts was magnanimous, and led to disagreement with officers of the garrison regiments and certain sections of the local society: he believed in allowing them to stand on an equal footing with the rest of the community when they had

proved they deserved it. He even occasionally appointed successful ex-convicts as local magistrates and invited select numbers to
his dining-table.

In 1819 William Wentworth's book *Statistical, Historical and
Political Descriptions of the Colony of New South Wales*, was published. In 1821 came James Dixon's *Narrative of a Voyage to New
South Wales and Van Diemen's Land in the ship Skelton during the
Year 1820 with Observations on the State of these Colonies and a
variety of information calculated to be useful to Emigrants*. These two
books greatly encouraged emigration. Another book about this
period which also had a considerable effect on public opinion was
Peter Cunningham's *Two Years in New South Wales*, published in
1827.

Peter Cunningham, a Dumfriesshire Scot, was a surgeon in the
Royal Navy with the post of superintendent of convict transport,
who travelled widely through New South Wales in 1820, 1821,
and 1822. In 1823 he was greatly impressed by the influx of free
settlers and in 1824 he himself took out a land grant for 1,200
acres on the Hunter River, which he named Dalswinton after his
family home. In August 1826 he wrote enthusiastically from
London:

> I have already expended £1,100 in stock and farming expenses
> and my stock alone by its increase equals that sum. I am also
> taking out a supply of agricultural implements . . . to the value
> of several hundreds more while 14 convicts are maintained on
> my land according to the letters of my friend Lt Ogilvie RN,
> who is managing my affairs in my absence.

Describing the countryside in his book the presence of Scottish
placenames was often noticeable, as was his enthusiasm:

> Some miles further on a road strikes off to the left towards
> Airds, Appin and Illawarra . . . the road towards Argyle runs
> straightforward from this . . . but by turning to the left after
> about four miles you come to Camden the great agricultural
> and sheep farm of Mr John Macarthur, to whom New South
> Wales owes so much as the patriotic introducer of the fine
> wooled sheep husbandry, from which in fact this Colony has
> derived nearly all the celebrity it now enjoys . . . New South

Wales and Merino wool are so intimately associated that I
never spoke of the first to a stranger but he started the subject
of Merino wool immediately as a sort of matter of course . . . It
is this product alone which has mainly elevated the name of the
Colony . . . to the proud station it now occupies.

One of the first settlers to consider himself Australian, he took a
pride in the country, referring to 'our colony – our roads – my
adopted country'. His knowledge of and enthusiasm for New
South Wales were very apparent, and his book soon communi-
cated them to the reader.

Between 1788 and 1800, only 70 Scots are estimated to have
been transported to Australia. By 1823 the number since 1788
was still only 855, or some 3½ per cent of the total number of
convicts transported at that date. During Macquarie's governorship, from 1810 to 1821, Scots received a sixth of the land
grants of 250 acres and more: by 1821 about a sixth of the free
settlers in Van Diemen's Land were Scots, and this soon rose to a
third. Throughout the 1820s there was a marked influx of small
tacksmen with Highland retainers, and similar gentlemen with
sums of from £2,000 to £3,000 – a considerable amount by the
standards of the day.

In 1822 the Edinburgh and Leith Australian Company was
formed to provide a regular shipping service for goods and
passengers between Leith and Australia. Its ninety-two partners
included shippers, bankers, lawyers, distillers, brewers, and merchants. Although primarily a shipping company, it was intended
to develop into a trading and loan company.

The arrival of the Company's first ship *Greenock* was awaited
with interest in 1823. About two-thirds of the merchants of
means and standing in Australia were Scots. Perhaps the most
important people concerned with this burgeoning trade, however,
were William Wemyss, assistant commissary in Sydney, and
Affleck Moodie who held a similar post in Hobart – both, of
course, of Scots birth.

One immediate result of the formation of the Company was a
considerable reduction in the cost of passages. They were able to
reduce costs from 70 to 50 guineas for first class, and from 50 to
30 guineas for steerage. The Company undoubtedly did a great
deal to encourage emigration, and between 1823 and 1831 they

appear to have carried some 900 passengers from Scotland to Australia.

The class of Scot – chiefly agricultural, professional, or commercial – was essentially reasonably well-to-do middle class. They were emigrating with a hopeful eye to the future rather than from desperation, and they appear to have had a considerable impact on their chosen country.

Exports from Scotland to Australia at this time included ale and whisky in barrels, Carron grates from the Carron ironworks, tartans, calicos, glass and pottery from the works at Leith and Portobello, anchors, ploughs, cart bodies, shawls, scarves, and linens. Amongst livestock, there were Ayrshire cows and bulls, Clydesdale stallions and mares. From Leith came soap, candles, and paper. From Edinburgh came thrashing machines (made by Moodie's, the Edinburgh manufacturers) and books by the thousand, including Sir Walter Scott's latest works.

In December 1826 the Hobart St Andrew's Club was formed. The members included the Scottish agent for the Australian Company, Charles McLachlan, and also the leading Scottish merchants, David Ker of the Roxburgh House Stores, Murray and Burns of the Caledonian Store, and William Walkinshaw and John C. Underwood. The first president was the surgeon, James Scott. The substantial Scottish clique in Hobart – merchants, farmers, and professional men – formed the bulk of the members, and the principal aims, apart from occasional dinners, were charitable.

From this period onwards, however, Hobart became less popular with Scottish emigrants, who turned instead towards New South Wales. One reason for this may have been Peter Cunningham's enthusiastic book: another the fact that transportation to Van Diemen's Land had not stopped, as it had been thought it would. Furthermore it was becoming obvious with the opening up of the interior that opportunities for newcomers were greater in many respects on the mainland.

The Australian Company of Edinburgh and Leith continued to be an important feature of the Australian economic scene. Ellis M. Scott, who came out in 1825 to act as Sydney agent, did much to save the Bank of New South Wales, of which he was elected a director and which in 1826 was in imminent danger of collapse. Acting on behalf of the Company, he supported the bank when it was hard pressed to the tune of at least £5,000, providing coin when this was required by selling merchandise for cash. Despite the economic depression in Scotland during the year 1826–7, the Australian Company's shares remained more or less sound at around £42–£47.

By 1828 the depression had begun to affect the Australian Company, to the extent that it started winding up its affairs. This was not, however, effectively achieved until 1830 and the final closure of the Company was not announced until 1831. Unable to sell their oldest ship *Triton* at £3,000, the Company ironically had eventually to send it to Quebec with immigrants for Canada.

There was something of a pause before the next phase of large-scale emigration to Australia. It was not until the mid-1830s that leading ironworks such as the Carron Company started to expand their antipodean trade. About the same time considerable imports of Australian wool began to arrive at the Scottish Border mills. The increasing destitution caused by the Industrial Revolution, as well as the two-way trade now developing, led to a tremendous spurt of emigration from all parts of Scotland, mostly working-class in character.

Previously emigration to Australia had principally been from the south-east, the Lothians, Edinburgh, Fife, and the Borders. Now the emigrants came also from the western Highlands, the south-west, Ayrshire, Dumfries, and Galloway, and from the north-east, Aberdeenshire, Angus, Moray, and Nairn. Even Orkney and Shetland supplied emigrants, as well as Inverness, Sutherland, and Ross and Cromarty. The availability of assisted passages after 1832 undoubtedly helped, but this was a period when emigration all round the world was increasing phenomenally, along with a rapidly rising birthrate throughout Britain.

In 1833 only 253 emigrants from Scotland sailed for Australia, as against 5,592 for the North American Colonies and 1,953 for the USA. In 1836 the total from all Scottish ports sailing to Australia fell to only 114; but in 1837 1,254 left for Australia against 2,381 for the North American Colonies and 1,130 for the USA. In 1831 the government had introduced assisted passages for female emigrants to New South Wales, and this was soon extended to mechanics; but Scotland was not greatly affected by this. In 1837, however, the colonial bounty scheme was extended to skilled agricultural workers, and this proved effective in Scotland, swelling the emigration figures to Australia at the expense of Canada and the USA.

Two books by contrasting divines were published in 1834, which may possibly have affected the issue slightly. In *An Historical and Statistical Account of New South Wales*, the Rev. John Dunmore Lang was flamboyantly optimistic about the country and its prospects. The Rev. Henry Carmichael, on the other hand, in his *Hints relating to Emigrants and Emigration . . . intending to display the advantages of New South Wales* was more careful, stating categorically that good prospects were only there for those with capital.

The Rev. John Dunmore Lang was born in Greenock in 1799. A minister in the Church of Scotland, he emigrated from Scotland to Sydney in 1823, when Sir Thomas Brisbane, the third Scottish Governor amongst the first six, had recently taken over from Macquarie. Lang managed to persuade Brisbane to finance a Presbyterian church and remained minister of it until his death in 1878, although with the advent of the Disruption in 1843 another Presbyterian church, St Stephen's, was built in Sydney.

Lang was a vital, if controversial, personality in the public life of New South Wales, and, as author of the book noted above, was always a strong advocate of emigration. A case he was fond of quoting was that of a Highlander, John McMillan of Skipness in Argyll, who was forced by poverty to act as a common porter in Greenock in the 1830s, and who arrived in New South Wales without a penny. Within seven years of his arrival in Port Phillip he had become a farmer with his own land and 400 head of cattle.

More relevant than either Lang's or Carmichael's publications was a small book edited by John Waugh and entitled *Three Years Practical Experience as a Settler in New South Wales*, which was published in 1838. This book was packed with information and sold eight editions in the first year. It contained extracts, never intended for publication, from a series of letters written home from New South Wales by the editor's son, David Lindsay Waugh, a young squatter in the Goulbourn district. In his first letter from Sydney, dated 25 June 1834, he wrote significantly:

. . . There are a great number of our countrymen here, and all very clannish. I have been introduced to almost all the respectable part of the community. I do not feel as in a foreign land at all and am very comfortable in my lodgings . . .

Although trained in law in Scotland, he was advised not to carry on with this as a career in New South Wales. In a further letter home he quoted the advice he had received in a letter addressed to a friend from an experienced Scottish emigrant who had already succeeded as a farmer:

> I will explain how he may invest his capital profitably while he is seasoning his fingers. He must not be above soiling them – he must think it no degradation to load a dung cart and drive a team of bullocks; in fact he must be a perfect farmer and he should and must learn if he wishes to prosper to be industrious; he must plough his own ground, sow and reap and afterwards not be above grinding it. When he can do all this . . . he will become a rich man. In seven years time with his capital (£300) judiciously managed he will be worth £1,500 per annum . . .

Following the advice in this letter, David Waugh took a job as a pupil-labourer on a successful Scottish emigrant's farm near Goulbourn, then a tiny settlement. He noted numerous Scottish neighbours:

> Three miles from us across the river Captain Currie's farm is possessed by two Allan's from Edinburgh; two miles below him is Mr Kinghorn's from Tiviotdale, 5,000 acres. The next is Captain Ross's splendid property and house and then Howie's and J. J. Moore's . . .

He was quickly promoted to managing the farm and recorded:

> In fact anyone with industry, sobriety and £10 in his pocket may succeed. The question is not how to get a living, but where are the best means of making a fortune. But rum-rum-rum-is all the go here – kills many and brings many to beggary. A sober man has a fortune at his feet . . .

On 31 July 1837, already successful, he wrote from his own farm:

My dear Father . . . You ask me about accommodation. I have a house of four rooms and detached kitchen and stores . . . I could build as many rooms as I pleased in the month . . . I have six convict servants [His two best men had been transported for 'happening' to sell a mare which had been stolen, and for poaching], one free shepherd, three with the sheep, two ploughmen, two bullock drivers, one boy who looks after the cattle and helps milk, one milkman, dairy man and overseer and his servant . . .

In November 1837 he recorded the increase in size of Goulbourn, now with 300 inhabitants, and noted:

We have now got a minister for Goulbourn – Mr Hamilton from the west country (Son of Mr Hamilton one of the ministers of Kilmarnock) . . . he has got above forty householder's names all Scotch to his call already . . .

Waugh's success was far from uncommon, for many of the Scots pastoralists in various parts of Australia started in a similar way and made good livings for themselves and their descendants. John Hood of Stoneridge in Berwickshire went out to visit his sons who had settled near Bathurst in 1841–2, and noted of a family retainer who had gone out with them: 'James is a good deal altered since he left Scotland. He wears his chin in colonial fashion with a beard as long as a Hebrew's which makes him look like a Cossack. His manner too is changed, more selfpossessed and more independent.' He also noted a Lachlan Mackay of Green Swamp, who had been a crofter on the estate of McLean of Coll and had set out from there with only £7. When Hood met him he was a prosperous stock-owner, well on his way to being a wealthier man than his old landlord.

Between 1836 and 1847 some 12,000 Scots emigrated to Australia, of whom about 10,000 went under the bounty schemes. For the first time there was a very considerable proportion of working-class Scots amongst the emigrants, now numbering about a sixth of the total as opposed to a tenth in earlier years. It should also be appreciated that the proportion of skilled craftsmen amongst the Scots emigrating at this time was proportionately far higher than in comparable shiploads of Irish, or even of English, emigrants. Not altogether surprisingly the standard of living in Scotland fell heavily during the 1830s and '40s, particularly in the western Highlands and in areas such as West Renfrewshire, where handloom weaving had become obsolete because of the introduction of new machinery in the mills.

The first Aberdeen Australian venture, intended purely as an investment group and known as the North British Australasian Company, was formed in 1839. This was still a time of boom and inflated prices in Australia, but this state of affairs was soon to end. Investing heavily in land at what seemed reasonable prices, the North British Australasian Company soon found itself in trouble.

The Scottish Australian Investment Company was more fortunate in that the boom had ended when it was formed in 1840. The directors also made a good choice of manager at the Australian end, for Robert Morehead, son of the Rev. Dr Robert Morehead, Episcopal Dean of Edinburgh, had a sound business and accounting background and soon proved himself. It was largely owing to him that the company was so successful. When the North British Australasian Company found itself in difficulties, Morehead loaned it money and in effect the second company saved the first from its disastrous investments. The flexibility of the Scottish Australian Investment Company, which dealt chiefly in mortgages, and the freedom given to Morehead as overseas manager, as well as his perspicacity and ability, combined with the fortunate timing of the company's arrival, were all factors which led to the success of this purely Scottish venture.

In 1850 Victoria was declared a separate colony and in 1851 the discovery of gold both there and in New South Wales resulted in a gold rush. 1851 was a disastrous drought year in Australia, and the gold rush was the saving of many who had thought themselves ruined by the weather. In 1852 some 100,000 emigrants landed at Melbourne, heading at once for the Victorian gold-fields: more than seven times the number recorded the previous year.

Not all the Scots who arrived in Australia were law-abiding characters. In 1838 a sixteen-year-old lad named Francis McCallum, reputed to be the son of a clergyman in Perth, was transported to Van Diemen's Land. In due course he took to the roads as a bushranger, calling himself Captain Melville. Some twenty years before Ned Kelly, Melville was the leading bandit of his day and many legends were told about him.

Perhaps typical of these was the occasion when he held up a wealthy squatter named Mackinnon in southern Victoria. Well dressed and well mounted, speaking with a good accent and behaving in a gentlemanly manner, as the story has it, he rode up to the Mackinnon homestead, left his horse with the groom and was shown into the drawing-room by the maidservant. Once face to face with Mackinnon, he drew a pistol and informed him that Captain Melville wanted an evening's entertainment from his daughters, whom he had heard played the piano and sang very well. Despite the squatter's expostulations Melville made it clear he was in earnest, and the impromptu evening duly went ahead with the bushranger, so it is said, playing the piano and singing an accompaniment to the daughters. It was all brought to an abrupt end by the arrival of the police, summoned by an alert servant. Melville, however, escaped by a back window. Such behaviour was not to save him when he was eventually caught in 1853, and he died in the hulks in 1857.

Melville – or McCallum – was certainly rash; to take on a Mackinnon was a dangerous game in south Victoria. There were many of the clan established there, and it was scarcely surprising that he received short shrift when tried at the court at Geelong. Today the rolls of Geelong Grammar School, famed as the Eton of Australia, still show a considerable preponderance of Mackinnons over other commoner names such as Smith.

So many Scots entered Australia, particularly South Australia, during the nineteenth century that it has been likened to an invasion. Their names read like a Scottish roll of honour: the Isbisters from the Orkneys; the Youngs from Shetland; the Macfarlanes from Caithness, one remove from Sutherland; the Macbeans, McLeans, the Robertsons of Struan, and many others from Inverness; the Riddochs from Aberdeen; the McCullochs from Perthshire. Among notable names from Fife were the Elders, Hays, Hughes, Murrays, McDouall Stuarts, the Fowlers, the Waites and numerous others; from the Lothians came the Melroses and Darlings; the Barr Smiths came from Renfrew; the Stirlings from Dumfries; the MacTaggarts from Argyll; the McKinlays and Milnes from around Glasgow.

Each of these names merits more than a mere mention and

much could be written about many of them, but of them all John McDouall Stuart should at least be briefly noted. Born in Fife in 1815, he emigrated to South Australia in 1838, entering the Survey Department. He first learned the principles of exploration under Captain Charles Sturt in 1844–5. In May 1858 and 1859 he completed his first inland exploration with one other companion. In 1860 he first tried crossing the continent from south to north, but failed. In 1861, he tried again and again was forced to turn back. Setting out once more in 1862, he was finally successful, but he never recovered from the effects of his privations and died in 1866. His journey across Australia and back in 1861–2 was of enormous value in opening up the country, and his monument remains the Overland Telegraph Line built along his route.

In the 1850s the Highlands and Islands Development Board was encouraging emigration to Australia rather than to Canada, on the principle that Australia was more suited to pastoral-minded Highlanders. From 1852 to 1857 they sent out nearly 5,000 Highlanders, the bulk of them going to Victoria. From the initial gold rush in 1851, until 1867, Australia, and particularly Victoria, was the part of the British Empire most attractive to emigrants. Since so many workers had been lured to the goldfields in search of an easy fortune, there were many jobs available.

The Scots were not only to provide Australia with farmers, bankers, politicians, merchants, business and professional men of all kinds from bankers to bushrangers, they also provided singers, poets, priests, and painters. There were Scots in literally every walk of life. If Captain Melville (or Francis McCallum) was one example of a sinner, Marie McKillop, born in Melbourne in 1842, was a fair example of a saint.

The daughter of Highland parents who had emigrated in 1838, Marie McKillop was always a devout Catholic. She started by setting up a free school for poor children in the outback and formed her own Order of St Joseph. She soon had a following of nuns wearing brown habits, familiarly known as Brown Josephs, engaged in teaching in schools for the poor. Although by nature mild and forgiving, she refused to be browbeaten by jealous and overbearing superiors in the Church. After many trials and misunderstandings she successfully established her Order as the Sisters of St Joseph of the Sacred Heart. Despite poor health, and

John McDouall Stuart, whose momentous crossing of the continent from Adelaide, via central Australia, to the north coast, in 1862, allowed the Overland Telegraph Line to be constructed along the route.

ultimately a stroke which left her in a wheelchair for the last seven years of her life, she was elected Mother General of the Order, dying peacefully in 1909. The Order now has 350 schools in Australia and New Zealand and some 2,000 sisters. She has been put forward for canonization as Australia's first saint.

David Mitchell, born in Angus in 1829, the son of a small farmer, was apprenticed to a stonemason before leaving for

Australia in 1852. Here he set up as a building contractor on the outskirts of Melbourne and was responsible for many notable buildings. In 1857 he married a Scotswoman from Angus and they had three sons and four daughters. By the time that David Mitchell died in 1916, on the same site where he had settled sixty-three years before, he had had the satisfaction of hearing his daughter, Dame Nellie Melba, singing all round the world and acclaimed as one of the finest opera singers of her day. One of Australia's best known poets, Mary Gilmore, was born Mary Jean Cameron near Goulbourn in 1863. She was created a Dame in 1936. Her poetry is human and intimate, deep-felt and diffuse. Perhaps typical, and revealing a Scottish background in that gift for the passionate expression of grief, is her 'Lament for the Waradgery Tribe':

> We are the lost who went,
> Like the cranes, crying;
> Hunted, lonely and spent,
> Broken and dying.

Another well-known Australian poet was Isobel Mackellar, daughter of Sir Charles Mackellar. She was born in Sydney, but her parents were both Scots. Her poetry is full of a love of her native land, and her poem 'My Country' is frequently sung in schools throughout Australia.

> I love a sunburnt country,
> A land of sweeping plains,
> Of ragged mountain ranges,
> Of droughts and flooding plains.

A man who must often have experienced the extremes epitomized in these lines, and who was a good example of the outstanding Scots pastoral pioneer, was George Melrose, born at Balerno near Edinburgh in 1806. He emigrated to Australia in 1839, and started as a sheep-farmer in the Mount Barker area, later moving to the Rhine. In 1847 he married Euphemia Thompson, daughter of a fellow-Scot from Kirkcaldy. He pioneered the land around Lake Victoria, but the government treated him very shabbily by giving the lease to someone else. However he built up a very successful station at Rosebank in the Rhine area, and died there in his eighty-eighth year in 1894, having determinedly survived good and bad years, and leaving five sons and three daughters to carry on in his footsteps.

A great-grandson of George Melrose was Charles James Melrose, killed in a flying accident in 1935 aged only twenty-two, but already by then a national hero. When he was only twenty he made a record round-Australia flight. Entering the England-to-Australia race, he set an unofficial record for the time from Australia to England of eight days nine hours; on the return flight from England to Australia, during the actual race itself, he came second, flying a Puss Moth, and winning £1,000.

Another interesting family of diverse talents were the Russells. Born in Fife in 1816, Peter Nicol Russell emigrated as a boy with his family in 1832. Trained as an engineer, he built up a successful engineering firm, and as a philanthropic benefactor of the University of Sydney he was knighted before his death in 1905. His nephew Peter John Russell, born in Sydney in 1859, became a well-known painter, an intimate of Van Gogh and Matisse. Having inherited money from his iron-founder father, he destroyed much of his work that he considered not good enough, but even so he is represented in many world capitals and art museums. He died in 1930, leaving five sons.

During the 1914–18 War the Australians rallied to the Empire cause. Thousands of Australians volunteered to fight in France, in Mesopotamia, and Gallipoli, in the trenches, in the navy, and in the air. The Scots-Australians, as ever, were prepared to form Scottish-affiliated regiments, and amongst these were the New South Wales Scottish, the South Australian Scottish, the Black Watch of Sydney, and the Gordon Highlanders of Melbourne.

There is an interesting indication of the popularity of the Scots in Australia at that time. With the wartime hysteria and anti-German feeling, several German families, considering them-selves in every way patriotic Australians, decided to change their names to others less obviously Germanic. Two families named Schubert chose Scottish names, one changing to Seaton and the other to Stewart. Inevitably, the women wore Stewart tartan to prove how Scots they were. Another family named Rattaey (pronounced Rat-eye) is said to have changed its name to Stirling

– but this might have been understandable even without the pressures of wartime hysteria.

No doubt these Schubert-Seaton-Stewarts also joined their local Caledonian Societies, for the overseas Scots have always had a remarkable ability to form such societies and the Australian Scots were no exception. Although some Scottish societies were almost certainly formed in the 1830s or '40s in Sydney or Melbourne, records do not start until the 1850s. The oldest recorded is the Highland Society of Maryborough, Victoria, formed in 1857 by pastoralists and gold-diggers. It has conducted a New Year's Day gathering ever since. A similar society formed in Geelong a year earlier lapsed in 1930. The Royal Caledonian Society of Melbourne, formed in 1858, lapsed in the 1870s and was reformed in 1884. The Highland Society of New South Wales was formed in 1877 by an amalgamation of a St Andrew's Scottish Benevolent Society and a Caledonian Society. The Royal Caledonian Society of South Australia was formed in 1881. Although each society is self-contained, there are in some states a Scottish Union to which they are all affiliated. In Victoria there were forty-four such societies affiliated to the Scottish Union in 1956.

As so often elsewhere, Scots were also closely associated with the printed word in Australia. The name of Syme, particularly, is almost synonymous with Australian newspapers. Ebenezer Syme, born in 1826 son of the parish schoolmaster in North Berwick, emigrated to Victoria in 1853. Dismissed from the *Argus* for his uncompromising views, he joined the newly established *Age*. In 1856 he became its proprietor in partnership with his brother David, but died four years later in 1860. His brother David, a year younger than he, then took charge. In 1879 he took his nephew Joseph Syme into partnership, but bought him out again in 1891 when Joseph wished to retire.

An unabashed crusader, David Syme exercised considerable influence through his paper. His eldest son, John Herbert Syme, took over on his death in 1908, and was followed on his own death in 1939 by Geoffrey Syme, his younger brother, as chairman. Oswald Julian Syme, the youngest son, became chairman in his turn, until 1964. Working closely with him was Hugh Randall Syme, elder son of John Herbert Syme, who volunteered for the Royal Navy in 1940 in a section rendering mines safe. He won the

George Medal in 1941, the bar in 1942, and the George Cross in 1943, becoming the most decorated Australian naval man serving. In 1946 he became general manager of the *Age*. He was chairman of the Australian Newspapers Council in 1959, and died in 1965.

With the outbreak of the Second World War in 1939, Australia once more joined Britain, along with the rest of the British Empire. On this occasion, however, Australia was soon fighting in defence of her own shores against the Japanese, and British naval and air forces were actively engaged in fighting in defence of Australia alongside Australians. Many British in the armed forces thus had their first glimpse of Australia, liked what they saw, and decided to emigrate after the war.

When the war was finally over in mid-1945, many British did in fact keep to that decision. In 1946 free passages for British ex-service emigrants were introduced. These were ended in 1954, although assisted passages continued and by 1955 half a million emigrants had gone from Britain to Australia. In 1956 when visiting Australia, the British Prime Minister, Harold Macmillan, claimed that since the war 250,000 emigrants from Britain had taken advantage of the assisted-passages schemes, and a further 250,000 had come out on their own.

In 1950 Robert Menzies, grandson of Scottish emigrants, became Prime Minister of Australia. Amongst his ministers were seven others of Scots descent, with names such as McBride, Cameron, Dickson, Weir. After sixteen successive years as Premier, and eighteen in all, having been awarded a well-deserved knighthood in 1963, Sir Robert Menzies retired in 1966.

Between 1955 and 1969 a million more British emigrants arrived in Australia and the total between 1945 and 1969 now amounted to 1,705,310. Since then the fairly continuous flow of emigrants from Britain has included a considerable quantity of Scots who continue, as elsewhere, to play a part out of all proportion to their numbers.

For example, in 1974 when Gough Whitlam took over as Premier, he appointed Sir John Kerr, Chief Justice of New South Wales, as Governor-General of Australia. Of Scottish descent, Sir John Kerr refused to allow a personal friendship between the two men to deter him from what he regarded as his duty. In December 1975 he acted within his powers as Governor-General and dismissed Gough Whitlam's government, appointing another Australian of Scottish background, Malcolm Fraser, as leader of the interim government. Malcolm Fraser was successful in the ensuing government elections, and in 1977 Sir John Kerr resigned at his own wish. Not surprisingly the Scots have a name for integrity in Australia, as elsewhere, and they have certainly served their adopted country well.

9

New Zealand

According to Maori tradition the first settlers in New Zealand came from Polynesia about the tenth century AD. The first European was Tasman in 1642, who charted part of the west coast, and following his discovery came the name Nieuw Zeeland. In 1769 Captain Cook annexed the islands for the Crown, but on his return the government disavowed his action since they could see no particular advantage in burdening themselves with more islands on the other side of the world. Apart from mapping the coastline meticulously, with only two obvious mistakes, Captain Cook released some pigs ashore, which in due course ran wild. Any wild pigs to this day are known as 'Captain Cookers', although much more probably descended from domestic pigs run wild from early settlements. Some could even be of Scottish origin.

The next seventy years saw scarcely any settlement worthy of the name. Numerous sealers made fortunes by decimating the vast seal population on the shores of both North and South Islands. Boatloads of sealers would be left by the crew of a ship which then went on elsewhere and returned to pick them up with their seals later. Sometimes the ship failed to return, and half-starved sealers were forced to seek help from the Maoris, or beg a lift from the next ship they saw.

The same lack of foresight which allowed the indiscriminate slaughter of the seal colonies also resulted in 'blackbirding', or press-ganging of natives, and the sale in Sydney of stuffed heads covered with tribal tattoos. This in turn led to ship's crews being attacked, killed, and eaten. The early missionaries sent out in 1814, however, were not ill-treated by the Maoris, but made no converts and generally came to bad ends through drink, women, or 'going native'.

By the 1820s there was a busy trade in flax for rope-making, which resulted in small ports and settlements developing, mainly

A Maori 'pa' or fortified village, from a drawing made during Captain James Cook's third voyage. Engraving by B. T. Pouncy, after an original by J. Webber.

set up by the agents. There was even a shipyard at Hokianga on the north-west end of North Island. The trade in kauri pine, a tree which grew sixty or eighty feet before branching, was worth several thousand pounds a year to Sydney firms. At the same time a series of whaling establishments were developed.

The centre for most of these activities was the Bay of Islands on the north-east end of North Island, opposite Hokianga. The local Maoris and settlers grew prosperous from victualling ships, and it is indicative of the increasing importance of the islands that in 1838 130 vessels called in the bay, of which thirty-six were from the United States, twenty-three were British, and twenty-one French, the remaining thirty being colonial, that is Australian or New Zealand.

There were undoubtedly Scots involved in all these activities, but there are insufficient records available to know exactly to what extent. Unfortunately, these commercial dealing were not always conducted within the law. In one notorious case in 1830 a Captain Stewart (presumably of Scottish origin) with his brig *Elizabeth*, agreed to transport a Maori chief and war-party down the coast to attack a rival, in return for a cargo of flax. After assisting in the battle, he shipped them back with the flesh of their enemies in baskets. The difficulty of obtaining witness in such cases usually prevented prosecution.

Certainly the bulk of the population of New Zealand in 1839 was judged by one Scot of forthright opinions in fairly damning terms. The Reverend John Dunmore Lang wrote: 'With a few honourable exceptions it consists of the veriest refuse of civilized society – of runaway sailors, of runaway convicts, of convicts who have served their term of bondage in one or other of the two penal colonies, of fraudulent debtors who have escaped from their creditors in Sydney or Hobart Town, and of needy adventurers from the two colonies, almost equally unprincipled.'

The main settlement at this time was Kororareka, the port for the Bay of Islands, which had an English Resident and an American Consul. The leading merchant, Gilbert Blair, was a Scot, and there were several sawyers and other merchants, a doctor, and a blacksmith. By the 1840s it had become quite a thriving community. Both a land company and a bank had been founded.

The Church Missionary Society had authorized the payment of £50 for maintenance on the birth of each child to a missionary. Land at this time could be bought for a few blankets or axes, so that £50 could buy a good-sized farm, and a large family could provide the proud father with an estate. Twelve missionaries were reputed to have had 84 children between them. The prominent and aptly named family of Fairbairn, of Mount Fairbairn, were the descendants of a Scots Church Missionary.

It was partly thanks to the behind-the-scenes activities of Edward Gibbon Wakefield and the New Zealand Company, which he was instrumental in forming, that New Zealand was officially recognized as a colony. As early as 1839 there was a New Zealand emigration society in Paisley, and it is clear that New Zealand had particular appeal for Scots from the earliest years. When the New Zealand Company decided to buy land and send a shipload of settlers without waiting for Colonial Office permis-

Settlers at Taranaki, New Zealand, building a hut.

sion, they were in fact merely anticipating events. In January of 1840 Captain William Hobson landed at the Bay of Islands and duly hoisted the Union Jack. At the Treaty of Waitangi he persuaded various Maori Chiefs to accept the sovereignty of the Queen, and thus became first governor of New Zealand.

The Maori way of life had already been greatly affected by the advent of the initial settlers. 'Civilized' diseases – syphilis and measles, amongst others – had severely attacked them. The sale of land, which by their laws belonged to all, was theoretically impossible, but by breaking their own laws and selling land in return for muskets they could pay off old scores. They were a

NEW ZEALAND COMPANY, EMIGRATION.

THE COURT OF DIRECTORS
NEW ZEALAND COMPANY

Are prepared to assist in Emigrating to their Settlements in New Zealand,

AGRICULTURAL
MECHANICS,
FARM LABORERS,

AND

Domestic Servants

Of good character, who will assist themselves by defraying a portion of the cost of their passage.

The Directors will receive Applications accordingly, until

WEDNESDAY, the 9th AUGUST,

From persons of the above description, desirous of proceeding on these terms by the Ship

AJAX

Appointed to Sail from the London Docks on

Monday, the 4th September next.

Further Particulars and Forms of Application may be obtained at New Zealand House.
By Order of the Court.

Thomas Cudbert Harington.

New Zealand House, 9, Broad Street Buildings, London,
24th July, 1848.

A. ECCLES, Printer, 101, Fenchurch Street, London

The New Zealand Company actively promoted emigration to the new colony, and offered assisted passages to prospective settlers.

warlike people who enjoyed fighting and made a point of eating their enemies. It required care and tact to deal with them effectively.

Following the recognition of New Zealand as a colony in 1840, some sixty-three ships arrived from Britain with settlers on board during the ensuing three years. Although only three of these are known to have sailed from Scottish ports, a considerable number of Scots seem to have sailed from English ports. It is probable that these Scottish settlers sailing from the south were organized initially by the New Zealand Company through agencies such as the New Zealand emigration society in Paisley. The first Scottish settlers to arrive were a shipload of 150, in 1839. They were accompanied by their own minister, the Rev. John Macfarlane, a Presbyterian minister from Paisley who could preach both in Gaelic and English. Amongst these settlers was one Donald McLean who was eventually to become the principal assistant to the Governor, Colonel Gore Brown, from 1855 to 1861, during which time he was to be directly responsible for the totally unnecessary Maori Wars, although he was to redeem himself subsequently by his part in ensuring a lasting peace.

In 1842 George Rennie, farmer and philanthropist, had the idea of forming a Scots Presbyterian colony in New Zealand, making full provision for the education and religion of the settlers. He interested the New Zealand Company in the plan, and was joined by a veteran of the Peninsular Campaign, Captain Wallace Cargill of the 74th Regiment of Foot, later to become the second battalion of the Highland Light Infantry. With the Disruption of the Church of Scotland in 1843, Rennie and Cargill approached the Free Church and in 1844 the Lay Association of the Free Church of Scotland negotiated with the New Zealand Company to buy 2,400 plots of sixty acres each, which were to be sold to emigrants at £2 an acre.

The first minister appointed, a nephew of the poet Robert Burns, was the Rev. Thomas Burns who had left the Church of Scotland in 1843 to join the Free Church. Along with 247 emigrants, he sailed from the Clyde in November 1847 and arrived in Otago Harbour in the South Island of New Zealand in April 1848 after a voyage lasting 117 days. Captain Cargill with ninety-seven emigrants on board another ship, sailed a few days earlier and arrived in March.

One of the more interesting arrangements on the voyage was that the surgeons provided for each ship received a bonus of £25 on arrival, less £1 for every death on board. Life on board ship was carefully arranged so that regular worship could be practised and the education of the children continued. Even so, in the shipboard conditions of the times the passengers must have naturally been very cramped and uncomfortable on a voyage of almost four months.

Once landed at Otago Harbour, the emigrants set up a temporary camp of huts on the site of what was to be named Port Chalmers, after the Rev. Chalmers, leader of the Disruption. The town which grew up on the site was eventually to be called Dunedin, the happy suggestion of William Chambers the publisher. (Less felicitous names proposed were New Edinburgh, Ossian, Mooretown, Wallacetown, and Edina.) The surveyor of the new town, named Kettle, visited Edinburgh with a view to naming the streets and modelling the town's plan on the capital of Scotland: there is thus a Princes Street, George Street, St Andrew's Street and Hanover Street, a Moray Place and York Place, a Royal Terrace and Heriot Row, apart from such evocative names as High Street, Hope Street, and Canongate Street.

The first church and the first school were in one and the same building, for to begin with there were not many settlers and growth was not rapid. By 1848 there were only 444, although another 130 arrived that year. Thereafter the growth of the settlement speeded up considerably. By 1854 there were 2,400 in Otago settlement, of whom 700 were in Dunedin. In the same year, the Presbytery of Otago was founded and the church flourished so well that by 1864 there were twenty-one parishes with their own ministers, sessions, and organization.

Fortunately for the settlers, relations with the Maoris, from whom the land had been bought, were friendly. Most of the Maoris on South Island were peaceful and had already been converted to Christianity. There was only one outbreak of violence in the very north of South Island in 1843. Otherwise, the Maori uprisings were entirely confined to the North Island.

Not all the Scots in Otago and its environs were, however, entirely law-abiding. One of the more outstanding figures of New Zealand folklore is James Mackenzie, who came from Ross-shire where he was born around 1820. Whether he came direct from

Centenary re-enactment, in 1948, of the historic arrival of Scottish settlers at Port Chalmers, Otago Harbour. A descendant of Captain Cargill, one of the two leaders of the emigrants, played the part of the Captain (centre, foreground) and wore the Captain's original blue bonnet.

Scotland with the Otago settlers, or whether he came via Australia where he had relatives (amongst them Alastair Mackenzie, High Sheriff of Melbourne) is not clear. Suffice it to say that he obtained a grant of one of the large tracts of land in the interior of Otago, dependent on his ability to stock it with sheep. Unfortunately he had neither sheep nor money. He did have, however, a well-trained sheepdog and he was accustomed to the mountains of his native Ross-shire.

He set out to explore the country and eventually discovered a pass through the Snowy Mountains into the lush pastures of the Canterbury Plains. Whether he was working entirely alone, or (as was later thought) in conjunction with others, he seems to have covered and partially explored some 12,000 square miles of rugged and virtually unknown mountainous terrain. Since his grant of land was conditional on his stocking it, and since he had no money, he felt his only course was to abstract stock from people like the Rhodes brothers, who owned the enormous Levels station extending from near the coast by Timaru to well into the foothills of the Southern Alps.

Once he had prospected his route, which is still known as Mackenzie's Pass, he set about systematically rustling sheep and cattle with the aid of a bullock and his dog. The bullock he loaded with his gear and when crossing rivers he hung on to its tail. The dog was trained to keep a flock of sheep or herd of cattle on the move without orders from his master. He had already removed an estimated 1,500 or 2,000 head of stock when he was caught with a flock of sheep by one of the Rhodes brothers' managers, accompanied by two Maori shepherds. After a struggle Mackenzie was tied up, but during the night he escaped and the Rhodes brothers put a price of £250 on his head. Five days later he was caught trying to find a ship near Lyttleton.

Knowing that he had already been condemned in a hostile press article, and faced with a jury and courtroom packed with sheep men, Mackenzie refused to plead when taken to court at Lyttleton near Christchurch accused of stealing a thousand sheep from Robert and George Rhodes. He refused to speak, even when offered a Gaelic interpreter, and was held to be 'mute of malice', not then an indictable offence. As sheep-stealing was not a hanging offence in New Zealand, he received the surprisingly light sentence of five years' imprisonment.

However, as he had not spoken in his own defence, James Mackenzie was able to plead a miscarriage of justice, and his plea was supported by Henry Tancred, the Lyttleton Sheriff, later

Chancellor of the University of Otago, and also by James Fitz-gerald, Superintendent of Canterbury Province, afterwards first Premier of New Zealand. Within nine months Mackenzie had also gained much public sympathy by escaping no less than three times, even when wearing 18 lb leg-irons. His petition to the Colony's Governor, Colonel Gore Brown, then proved success-ful and he walked out of Lyttleton gaol with a free pardon. In 1857 he sailed to Australia and vanished into the mists of time, but James Mackenzie deserves his place in the folklore of New Zealand as their one and only 'Highland freebooter'.

A more typical, and more law-abiding, Scotsman was Dr David Monro (1813–77) who arrived in New Zealand in 1842, having bought four allotments of land from the New Zealand Company for which he had paid £1,200. He settled near Nelson and was the first to introduce sheep from Australia. Within twenty years he had 14,000 sheep on 13,000 acres. He became a foundation member of the Company of Governors of Nelson College and was soon prominent in the political life of his adopted country. In 1853 he was elected to the House of Representatives, and from 1861 to 1870 he was Speaker. In 1856 he was knighted, and he died aged sixty-four in 1877. Despite his varied commitments and busy career, he had time occasionally to practise medicine, and several of his descendants also became doctors.

A Scot who arrived in 1852 was the Otago poet, John Barr. He was extremely delighted with his new life and wrote in praise of it, in the '50s:

When to New Zealand first I cam,
Poor and duddy, poor and duddy,
When to New Zealand first I cam
It was a happy day, sirs,
For I was fed on parritch thin,
My taes they stickit thro' my shoon,
I riggit at the pouken pin,
But I couldna mak it pay, sirs.

Nae mair the laird comes for his rent,
For his rent, for his rent,
Nae mair the laird comes for his rent,
When I hae nocht tae pay, sirs.

Nae mair he'll tak me aff the loom,
Wi' hanging lip and pouches toom,
To touch my hat and boo to him,
The like was never kent, sirs.

At my door cheeks there's bread and cheese,
I work or no, just as I please,
I'm fairly settled at my ease,
And that's the way o't noo sirs.

In the extreme south of the South Island, in the part later to be known as the province of Southland, the town of Invercargill was founded in 1857. In the same year 2,000 emigrants sailed from Scotland in eight ships, thanks largely to the promotion work of James Adam as emigration agent. He had been one of the original settlers of 1839, sent back by the Otago Provincial Council to take on the job of promoting emigration. Many years later, in 1876, he wrote his memoirs, *Twenty-Five Years of an Emigrant's Life in New Zealand*. He recorded:

'. . . a gentleman who thirteen years ago was a draper's assistant in the town of Kelso at a salary of probably thirty shillings a week, now owns the finest retail business in Dunedin, employs fifty hands and pays £250 weekly in wages . . . The enterprise of the Dunedin merchants has done much for the commerce and prosperity of Otago . . .
. . . Wearisome as eighty days sailing to New Zealand may appear in comparison with ten or twenty to America, yet I question if the advantages to the emigrant are not greater in the one case than in the other. The long voyage teaches the emigrant patience and economy in stowing himself and family afterwards in a small house. Habits of discipline are formed and the art of making the most of everything so that when he lands in his adopted country he is not easily put out with every little annoyance but on the contrary his long passage has only fitted and nerved him for difficulties yet to come . . .

In the exploration and surveying of the very difficult country on the west coast of South Island, Sir James Hector was one of the principals. Born in Edinburgh in 1843, he was later Director of the first Geological Survey of New Zealand and first Chancellor of the University of New Zealand, having previously found a way through the Rocky Mountains in Canada for the CPR. He was accompanied in New Zealand on his surveys by John McKerrow, followed later by Quinton Mackinnon and Donald Sutherland.

It is hardly surprising, in all the circumstances, that many parts of South Island have distinctly Scottish place names. Examples include Bruce, Little Paisley, Ettrick, Campbelltown, Oban, Clutha, Wallace, Roxburgh, Stirling and Fortrose. There are also many Bens among the mountains, including Ben Nevis, Ben Lomond, Ben More and a strange Maori-Scottish mixture in Ben Ohau. With sea lochs and mountain scenery, this was a familiarly Scottish-Highland background for the Scottish emigrants.

In 1857 Norman McLeod, ever in search of perfection (see page 120), left Australia after a brief stay, and arrived in Waipu in the far north of North Island, above Auckland, along with many of his faithful, if long-suffering, following from Nova Scotia. In that austere settlement the poet John Barr would have probably been even less happy than he had been back at his loom in Paisley with his landlord demanding the rent. Apart from the fact that Norman McLeod's followers still retained their native Gaelic, their firm observance of the Sabbath and their rigid adherence to doctrine would not have suited Barr's free and easy views on life. By the 1860s, however, McLeod's settlement had more than a thousand people, and in their own way they too were thriving.

By 1859 Donald McLean, earlier noted as having landed in 1839, had become both Chief Land Purchase Commissioner and also Native Secretary. As such he was Governor Gore Brown's chief assistant, but it was a most injudicious combination of offices since it appeared to the Maoris that the government was set on buying their land. Furthermore, McLean unfortunately deliberately adopted a scheme of not fully advising the Governor about important policy details. Even though the Assembly opposed many of the Governor's decisions, which had been inspired by McLean, war with the Maoris broke out in 1861.

Although Colonel Gore Brown was superseded as Governor by Sir George Grey in 1861 at the start of the Maori Wars, they were allowed to drag on unnecessarily long, until 1872. General Sir Alexander Cameron, commanding the troops fighting the Maoris, was markedly reluctant to risk his men's lives. Marching up the Taranaki coast in 1865, he kept almost entirely to the beach, and moved so haltingly that the Maoris named him 'the lame seagull'.

The white troops regarded the Maoris as very sporting enemies, but by 1866 all save one regiment had been withdrawn. In 1868 Sir George Grey himself was superseded, for opposing the Colonial Office once too often. Finally in 1870 the last regiment was withdrawn and it was left to the New Zealanders themselves to deal with the Maoris. By 1872 a peace had been negotiated which was to prove lasting. This was largely owing to the talents of Donald McLean, who had earlier resigned along with Colonel Gore Brown. Appointed Protector of the Aborigines and utilizing to the full his knowledge of the Maori language and customs, he had proved his worth and was knighted for his services. He died in 1878.

Fortunately the Maori Wars were restricted to North Island, for the discovery of gold in Otago in South Island, in 1861, resulted in a fresh influx of immigrants inspired by gold-fever. During the years 1861 to 1865, mostly as a direct result of this gold rush, total immigration amounted to approximately 93,000. Most of these immigrants inevitably went to South Island, although a small proportion did settle in North Island. Between 1871 and 1875, with the final ending of the tensions caused by the Maori uprisings, there was another substantial period of high immigration, with total figures of around 82,000. Thereafter the figures fluctuated, but on the whole the appeal of New Zealand to the Scots remained fairly strong.

With the peace of 1872 armed resistance was at an end, but one Maori Chief, Te Whiti, who believed (probably rightly) that McLean had granted them reserves before his death, launched a campaign of passive resistance, which proved effective for a while. In 1881 a military expedition led by the Native Minister, John Bryce, and his predecessor William Rolleston, who had resigned on the issue of using force, were met by 200 dancing and singing children when they went to arrest Te Whiti. Nevertheless he was gaoled indefinitely, without trial, under legislation which had been hurriedly passed. The youthful New Zealand poet of Scottish extraction, Jessie Mackay, wrote a parody of 'The Charge of the Light Brigade' on this event:

When can their glory fade:
Oh! The wild charge they made!
New Zealand wondered
Whether each doughty soul
Paid for the pigs he stole,
Noble Twelve Hundred!

As everywhere overseas, it seems inevitably, the Scots broke into print – as poets, like Jessie Mackay, or as journalists. Certainly the New Zealand newspapers had their full quota of Scots. William Berry (1839–1903) worked on *The Scotsman* before emigrating in 1864, eventually becoming editor of the *New Zealand Herald*. James Walter Bain (1841–1899), born in Edinburgh and a compositor by trade, became owner of the *Southland News* and *Southland Times*. David Bell, a native of Dunfermline, first emigrated to Queensland in 1883, where he was under-manager of a newspaper. On arriving in New Zealand he became manager of the *Lyttleton Times* and chairman of the *Timaru Post*. Many others were connected with newspapers and journalism in both North and South Islands.

One Scot, however, whose work was as far-reaching as any in New Zealand, was Thomas Brydone (1837–1904), who was born in West Linton, and became interested in the dairy industry and in frozen meat. He was a partner with George Davidson, another Scot, in the New Zealand and Australian Land Company, and in 1882 they shipped the first consignment of frozen meat from New Zealand (from Port Chalmers) to London, on a ship appropriately named the *Dunedin*. Another notable Scottish emigrant cattle- and sheep-breeder of the same period was Walter Buchanan, who also went into the frozen meat industry. Few aspects of farming were more calculated to boost New Zealand's exports.

A Scot who was prominent in the politics of New Zealand during this period was Sir Robert Stout (1844–1930). A Shetlander, born in Lerwick, he went out to New Zealand in 1864 to become a teacher, but instead read law and became at first a lecturer in law at Otago University. Turning from law to politics he became a left-wing Liberal MP from 1875. From 1884 to 1887 he was Prime Minister, and from 1899 to 1926, Chief Justice.

Perhaps even more memorable in New Zealand, however, was one of his radical supporters, John Mackenzie, a Ross-shire

Port Chalmers, South Island, in the days of clipper ships: from this port the *Dunedin* sailed in 1882, carrying the first cargo of frozen meat to Britain.

crofter born in 1838 who emigrated to Otago in 1860 with an understandable hatred of landlords, having himself been a victim of the Clearances. In 1891 he was appointed Minister of Lands, and the legislation he passed included measures whereby the Government reserved the freehold of all Government lands sold. It also gave the Government power to take over, at the owner's valuation, the land of those who complained that their assessment was too high, and provided for the compulsory repurchase of land, with power to insist on genuine residence and cultivation of land, thus outlawing absentee landlords. New Zealand had entered into a socialist economy ahead of any other nation.

This did not prevent a considerable outburst of nationalistic feeling when the Boer War broke out, and volunteers were not hard to find for regiments sent across to repress the Boers. Nor was there any lack of volunteers in the First World War. Amongst other regiments, the New Zealand Scottish were noteworthy. More than 100,000 men served overseas, as much as 10 per cent of the population of only a million; and the cost was dear in the extreme. The New Zealand casualties totalled 58,000 – or one in every seventeen of the population; fantastically enough, higher even than those of Belgium which was a battlefield. This was the formation of a nation.

A man who became an MP in 1918 was another left-wing Scot,

Peter Fraser, born in Ross-shire in 1884. In 1908 he joined the Independent Labour Party in London, and in 1910 he emigrated to New Zealand, where he soon became a prominent supporter of the Socialist party. After becoming an MP, he served in Parliament and in various government posts until appointed Prime Minister in 1940, continuing as Prime Minister throughout the war until 1949.

In the Second World War, once more, the New Zealanders came to the support of the Empire, and again the cost was high. On this occasion the war was brought nearer home with the presence of the Japanese in the Pacific. The concept of the British Commonwealth of Nations was to mean a lot to New Zealanders after the war, with the gradual shedding of the Empire.

The formation of the Common Market in Europe, and the United Kingdom's entry into it, meant that the ties with New Zealand, as with Australia, were in many ways diminished. Yet as far as Scotland is concerned, this is not entirely the case. For example there are well over a hundred pipe-bands in New Zealand, and Burns Clubs and many other associations with Scotland are maintained. There are numerous Clan Societies and Caledonian Societies in both North and South Islands.

An example, with a slightly unusual twist, is to be found in Waipu where Norman McLeod and his followers finally settled after leaving Nova Scotia. This Caledonian Society has held a New Year gathering every year since its formation in 1871 and lists its objects in much the expected manner, with one significant variation: 'To keep up the customs, traditions, and language of the mother country, Highland dancing, music, games, etc, and to assist any immigrants from the Highlands of Scotland, *or from Nova Scotia*, who settle in Waipu and are in need of help.' Any Scots following in Norman McLeod's footsteps and emigrating first to Nova Scotia before moving on to Waipu would no doubt be doubly welcomed.

As with Australia, there were free passages for ex-servicemen after the 1939–45 War, and these also ceased in 1954, although assisted passages generally continued for some time afterwards. Between 1947 and 1956, 100,000 British immigrants arrived in New Zealand, of whom 31,000 were assisted, though exact figures showing the proportion of Scots amongst these are not available.

From 1962 until 1967, Brigadier Sir Bernard Fergusson was Governor-General. A member of a distinguished Ayrshire family with a long record of public service, Brigadier Fergusson, a past Colonel of the Black Watch, had served with distinction in the Chindits during the war. There was a particular sense of fitness about his appointment since his father, General Sir Charles Fergusson, had been Governor-General between the wars.

In 1972 there were 15,000 immigrants to New Zealand, mostly British; and in 1973 this rose to 25,000. Careful to regulate the number of immigrants to suit the population, which by this time was around 3 million, New Zealand placed a temporary ban on immigration in 1975. This has, however, since been removed.

Amongst those Scots emigrating since then, and unwittingly following the example of Norman McLeod by emigrating first to America, was Dr Randall Allardyce, whose grandfather had left Strathaven in 1910 for Indiana (see p. 110). After specializing in heart-surgery at Edinburgh, and marrying a Scots girl, Dr Allardyce was offered a senior post at Christchurch Clinical School in the University of Otago and moved to Canterbury in the mid-1970s.

Any Scot emigrating to New Zealand, whether direct from Scotland, or, like Dr Allardyce and Norman McLeod, at one remove, will find a large preponderance of fellow Scots. In no other country overseas will the emigrant Scot feel quite so instantly at home, for not only is the juxtaposition of rivers, lochs, mountains, and sea highly reminiscent of Scotland, as well as many of the place-names, but New Zealand is also a small, proud, and independent nation.

10

India and Africa

The eighteenth century was the time when the East India Company's rule was paramount in India. It was the time when corrupt nabobs could amass fortunes in ways scarcely likely to endear the British to the Indians, but which were in fact exactly what they expected from their own rulers. With the arrival as Governor-General in 1798 of the Marquis of Wellesley, then Lord Wellington, friend and confidant of Pitt, the end of the Company rule was in sight. In fact the Company's commercial monopoly was not abolished until 1813, and the entire administration was not passed to the Crown until 1858, but by the start of the nineteenth century a new approach to India was beginning.

By this time the Scots were well established in India in the East India Company's service, as a glance at the registers in Haileybury (once the old East India Company's college) will show. As administrators, soldiers, and cadets they were already to the fore. Throughout the continuing years of British rule in India they were to be conspicuous, whether as administrators from the rank or Viceroy or Governor-General downwards, as soldiers, merchants, engineers, or judges – indeed, in every walk of life.

Wellesley's ambitious policies of expansion and continual wars exhausted the patience of the Company directors at home. He was recalled in 1804 and replaced by Lord Cornwallis, who died very shortly after his arrival in the country. A brief interregnum preceded the arrival of Lord Minto who was appointed Governor-General in 1806 and governed successfully from 1807 to 1813. The eldest son of Sir Gilbert Elliot, third baronet, of a distinguished Scots Border family, Lord Minto had been created Baron Minto for his services as Governor of Corsica. As Governor-General of India he consolidated all Wellesley's conquests without further fighting. Two of his most successful administrators were also Scots, Mountstuart Elphinstone and Sir John Malcolm, both friends of Wellesley.

Mountstuart Elphinstone (1779–1857), fourth son of Lord Elphinstone, of an old East Lothian family, entered the East India Company Service at the age of seventeen. In 1808 Lord Minto appointed him first British envoy to the Shah of Afghanistan in Kabul. In 1815 he published a book entitled *An Account of the Kingdom of Cabul*, which proved very popular. After being Resident in Poona, he became Lieutenant-Governor of Bombay in 1819 and remained there until 1827. He was the founder of State Education in India, and Elphinstone College in Bombay was named after him. On his retirement in 1829 he wrote a *History of India*, published in 1841. He twice refused the offer of the Governor-Generalship of India after his return home.

Sir John Malcolm (1769–1833) was born near Langholm on the Scottish borders, son of a farmer three of whose sons were knighted. At the age of twelve he received a cadetship into the Indian army. A successful linguist, he learned to speak Persian well, and at Seringapatam he became friendly with General Sir Arthur Wellesley, afterwards the Duke of Wellington. He acted successfully as envoy to the Persian Court on behalf of Lord Wellesley in 1800. In 1808 he was again sent on a mission to Persia by Lord Minto, although this time without success. He was knighted in 1811, and in 1815 he wrote a two-volume *History of Persia*. After holding various other posts he was appointed Governor of Bombay in 1827, where he was responsible for many useful reforms. He left India in 1830, and became an MP on his return home, but died in 1833.

Another influential Scot in India during this period was Sir Thomas Munro (1781–1827), who spent most of Lord Minto's term of Governor-Generalship on furlough at home. Born in Glasgow, he served as an infantry cadet in Madras in 1789, seeing action against Hyder Ali and Tippoo Sahib. He then spent some time supervising ceded areas of Hyderabad, before returning home for seven years. After some further valuable military service he was appointed Governor of Madras in 1820, and the systems of revenue assessment and administration which he introduced there remained unaltered for the reminder of the century. In 1827, like so many others, he died of cholera.

Not all the Company's European officers in charge of sepoy regiments were of such high calibre. The Earl of Mar and Kelly kept a diary in the 1830s in which he portrayed his brother officers, most of whom seem to have been fellow Scots. Unless he had been soured by years in the tropics, they cannot have been of a very high standard. He wrote:

> Carter . . . was adjutant . . . born and educated in Edinburgh . . . He is a man of excellent education and used, until his imagination grew marked of late, to be possessed of sound judgement. He was always eccentric, but until he quite withdrew into himself from the world he was not only much liked but looked up to in the Regiment. Now he joins in nothing and is ill and useless to the corps . . .
>
> Mr Muir is a regular long-headed *canny* Scotchman. No man knows better how to look after his own interests. His manners are exceptionally vulgar, particularly so to his juniors in rank; sometimes very overbearing to those who will allow it, but cringing to those from whom he has anything to gain . . . He is a useful member of the corps but not an *ornament* . . .
>
> Hunter, or Little Bob, as he was generally called, is a quiet, good, harmless little fellow. Of no use and of no harm . . .
>
> Andrews; a strange compound, generally speaking gentlemanly in his manners, but not polished and sometimes rude. A remarkably clever musician, plays violin and flute in first rate style, draws neatly, an excellent billiards and cricket player, neat-handed writer and beautiful lady-like hand, exceptionally silly, weak and ignorant, active in body, slothful in mind . . . Very foppish in his dress and yet exceptionally dirty in his person. A young lady once very properly called him 'the dirty dandy' . . .

These opinions make it easy to understand how, in the conditions in India of those days, men could easily turn to quarrelling. This was especially so where important issues were at stake. A good example was a difference of opinion between two Scots, Sir Alexander Burnes and his superior Sir William MacNaghten, which ended in both their deaths.

Sir Alexander Burnes (1805–1841) was born in Montrose, joined the East India Company army in 1822, and being a natural linguist was appointed interpreter in Persian and Hindustani. He was then soon assistant to the political agent in Cutch. In 1831 he was sent to Lahore and travelled through Afghanistan, across the

Hindu Kush, to Bokhara and Persia, and in 1834 he published an account of his travels which sold well. In 1836 he was sent on a mission to Kabul. His advice to the Governor-General, Lord Auckland, was opposed to that of his superior Sir William MacNaghten, whose policy was to try to placate the Afghan chiefs with subsidies. Despite this conflict, and his frequent adverse reports on the success of MacNaghten's policy, Burnes was appointed political agent in Kabul. He carried on and remained at his post, but was assassinated in November 1841. Subsequently it was discovered that some of his despatches had been altered to convey the opposite of what he had intended.

Sir William Hay MacNaghten (1793–1841) was born the second son of Sir Francis MacNaghten, judge of the supreme courts of Madras and Calcutta. In 1809 he went out to Madras as a cadet and, having been born in India, found the language came naturally to him. When Lord Auckland became Governor-General in 1837, he acted as his close adviser. He differed strongly, as noted above, with the military authorities in Kabul, and in particular with his subordinate Sir Alexander Burnes over his policy of trying to placate the Afghan chiefs. After Burnes's death he himself was assassinated while trying to negotiate with Akbar Khan – in December of the same year, 1841. His policy was undoubtedly wrong, but whether it was he who went to the lengths of altering Burnes's despatches will probably always remain unknown.

One of the more important Scots briefly in India at this period was Thomas Babington Macaulay (1800–1859), later Lord Macaulay. An MP in 1830, hard-pressed for money, he was offered a seat on the supreme council of India worth £10,000 a year, and sailed in 1834 for Calcutta. He was appointed President of the Commission to enquire into the jurisprudence, and eventually produced what was to become the penal code of India, a model of its kind. It was said of it that: 'It reproduced in a concise and even beautiful form the spirit of the law of England, in a compass which by comparison with the original may be regarded as absurdly small.' In 1838 Macaulay returned to England, but in his Indian service of only four years he had left his mark.

The next Scot to be Governor-General of India was James Andrew Broun Ramsay, Marquess of Dalhousie (1812–1860), who was born at Dalhousie Castle, the family seat in Midlothian.

Thomas Babington Macaulay (later Lord Macaulay) by J. Partridge. In his four years in India, 1834–38, Macaulay produced the country's penal code, based on that of Britain and a model of its kind.

After a brief career in Parliament he accepted the Governor-Generalship of India and the Governorship of Bengal in 1848. By the time he left, in 1856, he had accomplished more than any Governor-General since Wellesley, and his innovations were very much more far-reaching.

He was forced to fight in the Punjab, which was annexed to the Crown, and again in Burma, which was also then annexed. He was responsible too, for the annexation of Oudh because of the excesses of its ruler. It was, however, principally for his initiation of public works, for the building of canals and roads, and the laying down of the first railways, that he is remembered. By the end of his tenure of office, the route to India was by steamship via the Red Sea. He had instituted cheap postage and introduced the telegraph. He also foresaw, and warned the government of, the danger of the Mutiny which followed in 1857.

Prominent in the administration while he was Governor-General were the three Lawrence brothers, Sir George Lawrence, Sir Henry Montgomerie Lawrence (killed at the siege of Lucknow in 1857), and, above all, John Laird Mair Lawrence (1811–1879), afterwards Lord Lawrence, whose mother was a collateral descendant of John Knox. The latter, as Sir John Lawrence, invested Delhi in 1857 with all the troops he could raise from the Punjab, and was finally successful in retaking the city from the mutineers. He returned home in 1860 hailed as 'the saviour of India'.

During the Mutiny the Highland Brigade, already famous for its exploits in the Crimea, was shipped to India under its old Commander Sir Colin Campbell. The skirl of the pipes and the feats of the Highland soldiers became renowned throughout India. At Lucknow alone the 42nd Highlanders (the Black Watch) and the 93rd (the Sutherland Highlanders) won fifteen VCs between them.

In 1862 Lord Elgin was appointed Viceroy, but after a very short period in office he died unexpectedly in 1863. Recalled from retirement, Sir John Lawrence served as Viceroy from 1864 to 1869, consolidating all the borders of India and improving the internal administration of the country. On his return to England in 1869 he was created Lord Lawrence of the Punjab.

Prominent also at the defence of Lucknow was Lord Napier (1810–1890), then General Napier, who was born in Colombo and joined the Royal Engineers in 1826. After a lengthy career in India as an engineer, he ended up as Commander-in-Chief in 1870. Following a long and gallant career he was appointed Field Marshal in 1883. His namesake, Lord Napier and Ettrick (1819 –1898), son of the Lord Provost of Edinburgh, Alexander Napier,

Uniforms of the 78th Highlanders in India, 1852, by R. Simkin. Highland regiments played a conspicuous part during the Mutiny of 1857.

entered the diplomatic service and was appointed Governor of Madras in 1866. In 1872 he acted briefly as Viceroy on Lord Mayo's assassination. On Lord Northbrook's appointment he returned to England where he was made a baron for his services.

Throughout the latter half of the nineteenth century the Scots continued to be prominent in the government and general administration of India. From 1894 to 1899 the Viceroy was the ninth Earl of Elgin (1894–1912), son of the eighth Earl, who had held the post in 1863–3. Somewhat over-cautious, his ministry was most memorable for the frontier risings of 1897–8 which were allowed to escalate, because of hesitation on the part of the government, until the Afridis in revolt seized the Khyber Pass. This necessitated the Tirah Expedition to suppress them.

From 1905 to 1910, Lord Minto was Viceroy. Gilbert John Elliot, fourth Earl of Minto, was great-grandson of the first Lord Minto who had been Governor-General from 1807 to 1813. By the early twentieth century, however, the imperial image in India had begun to change, and by using tact rather than drive Lord Minto succeeded in putting over reforms which were the first transitional moves towards self-government.

The First World War brought many Indian regiments out to fight in Mesopotamia and Europe. Frequently officered by Scots, some of whom by this time were Anglo-Indians of third and fourth generations (though still regarding themselves as Scottish first and foremost), these regiments had evolved traditions as proud as many of those in Britain. Skilled in frontier warfare during the years of British rule, they were a useful fighting force by any standards.

The inter-war period saw further demands for Independence from the politicians in India. Another Scot, the Earl of Linlithgow, was Viceroy during the critical years from 1936 to 1943. Although he may have lacked the imaginative spark of brilliant leadership, he was not afraid to control and direct during the difficult wartime years, nor was he ever likely to show infirmity of purpose in the face of threats. He proved able to face up to a task that might have daunted many lesser men.

Lord Linlithgow's successor was another Scot, Field-Marshall Lord Wavell, who served as Viceroy from 1943 to 1947, being in effect the last real ruler of India. He was a great and inspired, if unobtrusive, leader, with a powerful mind, who carried out his work with tact and brilliance. Considering their past share in the administration of India, with seven Viceroys out of twelve, it was entirely fitting that it should have been two Scots, who brought the British rule in India to its closing stages.

Since then, of course, many Scots have served as advisors, as doctors, as missionaries, and in many other ways in India, Pakistan, and Bangladesh, as well as in Burma and Nepal. There are also many Anglo-Indians and Eurasians of Scottish blood still living in the sub-continent. In addition many unremembered graves attest to Scots who laid down their lives serving an ideal and passing on skills, beliefs or knowledge in the process.

Compared with their interest in India, the British were curiously indifferent to Africa. Presumably once the Cape route was in British hands, it was felt that commitments in India were too great to involve Britain much more deeply in Africa. In any event the Scots in Africa, understudies of the English as in India, were primarily explorers, missionaries, and merchants, rather than colonizers and administrators.

The earliest Scottish explorer of Africa was James Bruce, 'The Abyssinian' (1730–94), who was Consul in Algiers in 1763. In 1768 he sailed up the Nile to near Aswan and crossed the desert to the Red Sea; in 1770–1 he explored Abyssinia and the waters of the Blue Nile. When he returned and published an account of his travels, he was generally thought to be romancing. Soon afterwards came Mungo Park, born in Selkirk in 1771. In 1795 he explored the Niger through Gambia, and on a second expedition he died near Timbuctoo in 1806.

There were a certain number of Scottish settlers in Africa, it is true, but Canada, Australia, and New Zealand almost always proved of greater appeal. Amongst the earliest British settlers in Africa were some who had come to the Cape Colony as soldiers and decided to stay. One of these was a Glaswegian named Robert Hart, who first arrived with the British forces stationed there in 1795. He returned again in 1807 and decided to stay on when his period of service ended. He was among the first to introduce merino sheep there. Another Scot who came as a soldier in 1806 was John Graham. He married a Dutch settler's daughter and decided to stay. He died in 1821, but his descendants played their part in the life of South Africa.

Along with the soldiers went missionaries, as an account of the religious zeal of the 93rd or Sutherland Highlanders, stationed at the Cape from 1805 to 1814, indicates:

Anxious to enjoy the advantages of religious instruction agreeably to the tenets of their national church, and there being no religious service in the garrison, except the customary one of reading prayers to the soldiers on parade, the men of the 93rd formed themselves into a congregation, appointed elders of

Mungo Park, born in Selkirk in 1771, was one of the earliest Scottish explorers of Africa. Engraving by T. Dickinson, after a drawing by H. Edridge.

their own number, engaged and paid a stipend (collected from the soldiers) to a clergyman of the Church of Scotland, who had gone out with the intention of preaching to the caffres [*sic:* kaffirs] and had the Divine Service performed agreeably to the ritual of the Established Church . . .

It seems likely that the clergyman in question was sent out by the London Missionary Society, which was founded in 1795 and first sent missionaries to Africa in 1799. Although the Edinburgh and Glasgow Missionary Society was founded in 1796, it sent out no missionaries until 1826. The Church of Scotland itself did not start despatching missionaries until 1829. A certain William Anderson, son of an Aberdonian living in London, was the first missionary sent out to the Cape by the London Society, arriving in 1800 and staying until 1818; it may conceivably have been he who also served with the Sutherland Highlanders as their minister.

Since there was a close affinity between the Dutch Reformed Church and the Scottish Presbyterian Church a rather unusual situation arose in that Scottish ministers were able to serve both Churches. The first Scottish minister actually to serve as a pastor in the Dutch Reformed Church was Dr George Thom in 1812. A number of others came out at intervals until as late as the 1860s to follow his example, such names as Colin Fraser, Andrew Murray, James Macgregor, and Alan Nicol being notable. Since most of them married Dutch wives, adopting the language of their flocks and rearing large families, they introduced a moderating influence over the years on the extreme anti-British propagandists which should not be underestimated. It was not until 1829 that the first Scottish Presbyterian Church was founded by the Rev. James Adamson.

The first organized Scottish group of any size to settle in the Cape Colony appears to have been arranged by an Orcadian, Benjamin Moodie, who had settled in the Swellendam area. In 1817 he arranged for a party of some 200 Scots to come to Cape Town on the condition that they indentured themselves to him for a period of three years. A similarly organized party was arranged in 1818 by two other Scots in the Cape Colony. This led in turn to further emigration, since these settlers soon did well for themselves and encouraged others to follow their example.

In 1819 the British government voted £50,000 to encourage emigration to South Africa, with a promise of 100 acres of land rent-free for ten years. Between 3,000 and 4,000 immigrants took advantage of this offer and were mostly sent to the Albany area to act as a buffer against attack by the natives. Most of these settlers found the conditions discouraging and numbers of them eventually retired to Cape Town. There do not appear to have been many Scots in this group, but a ship from the Clyde with some 200 would-be Scottish emigrants on board caught fire en route, with considerable loss of life.

Among those Scots who eventually landed in 1820 was Robert Pringle from the Scottish Border country, with his four sons. One of the sons, Thomas Pringle, had been editor of *Blackwood's Magazine* and was also an author and poet. He described his experiences in the Cape Colony in *Narrative of a Residence in South Africa*, and also wrote much verse. Although a fairly excruciating poet at times, he depicted the scene in Africa in those early days in glowing lines which catch the amazing silence of the open spaces, the marvellous abundance of animal life, the savage weirdness of the natives, and the wild spirit of adventure of those early colonists. His best-known poem starts:

Afar in the Desert I love to ride,
With the silent Bush-boy alone by my side;
Away – away from the dwellings of men,
By the wild deer's haunt, by the buffalo's glen;
By valleys remote, where the oribi plays,
Where the gnu, the gazelle and the hartebeest graze;
Where the kudu and eland unhunted recline,
By the skirts of grey forests o'erhung with wild-vine . . .

At the same time as the Pringles came William Elliot, who founded a school in Cape Town in conjunction with another Scot named Andrew Duncan. James Innes from Banffshire, who had graduated at Aberdeen University, was appointed Superintendant-General of Education in the Cape Colony in 1821, and in 1822 he landed with half a dozen fellow Scots whom he had recruited as schoolmasters. In 1830 he was associated with John Fairbairn and the Reverend James Adamson in the foundation of the South African College, and in 1841 he arranged for the immigration of a further seven schoolmasters from Scotland. He continued as Superintendent of Education until 1859, so that all in all the Cape Colony education had a decidedly Scottish flavour.

Thomas Pringle, regarding the 1820 settlement in Albany as a mismanaged failure, was amongst those who withdrew to Cape Town. There he obtained a post as government librarian. He also, in conjunction with John Fairbairn, published a *South*

African Journal, highly critical of the government's mismanagement. He was summoned before the Governor-General, Lord Charles Somerset, who was something of a despot, and soundly berated. He refused to publish further editions without freedom to write as he thought fit, but this was not granted.

The first independent newspaper in South Africa was, almost inevitably, produced by a Scot, George Greig. Called *The South African Commercial Advertiser* it first appeared in 1823. George Greig, as printer and proprietor, was joined by Thomas Pringle, who, as an experienced editor and striving poet, was no doubt a natural journalist. Along with these two was John Fairbairn. Initially they had something of a struggle to establish the freedom of the Press, for when they were somewhat critical of the government their printing presses were confiscated and George Greig was banished. He, however, was soon actively campaigning against this in Britain and a memorial complaining of Somerset's actions was sent to the King in Council, no doubt contributing to his recall in 1826. By 1828 the freedom of the press in South Africa was confirmed by the Secretary for the Colonies – yet another Scot, Sir George Murray.

From 1836 to 1840 the Boer settlers engaged in the famous Great Trek, emigrating from the Cape Colony to beyond the Orange River and then on beyond that into the Transvaal, where they finally established themselves. The reasons behind the Boer discontent were threefold. Firstly they objected to the Emancipation of Slavery Act of 1834, under which they had to give up their slaves for totally inadequate compensation. Secondly, they refused to accept the principle of equality with the black man inherent in the British treatment of the kaffirs. Thirdly, they thought the British treated the kaffirs preferentially to them. While the British immigrants of the 1820s were still struggling to establish themselves, the Boers were in a state of considerable indignation and left the colony accordingly.

From the Boer viewpoint, the British government seemed to be blowing hot one moment and cold the next. They seldom understood the Boer position. In 1842, for instance, Mr Justice Menzies (clearly a Scot), one of the Cape Colony judges, proclaimed the territory beyond the Orange River to be British. This was refuted by the Governor, Sir George Napier, who was shortly succeeded by another Scot, Sir Peregrine Maitland. Within a year he, in turn, had been followed by Sir Harry Smith. In the circumstances it is scarcely surprising that the Boers were bewildered. British support of the neighbouring tribes resulted in endless dissension and open warfare.

From 1824 onwards a number of settlers, mostly Boers, had arrived in Natal. More arrived in 1834, and an attempt was made to declare it separate from the Cape Colony. In 1843 it was recognized as a colony, although still dependent on the Cape Colony, and it was not until 1856 that the government eventually agreed to recognize it as a separate Colony in its own right.

After the initial recognition in 1843, British settlers began to consider the prospects in Natal for the first time. In 1846 Hugh Maclean, the owner of the island of Coll on the west coast of Scotland, sent out his eldest son to look at Natal with a view to its general suitability for immigration. In 1849 a party of emigrants 127 strong sailed from Glasgow; most were from Clydeside, although some were from further afield. In 1850 they were joined by two Free Church ministers – William Campbell, who had been the Free Church minister in Alexandria at the foot of Loch Lomond, and Charles Scott, who had been minister for Peterhead in Buchan until the Disruption, when he had changed to the Free Church and hence had lost his charge.

The Wakefield system of assisted passages had been introduced in the 1840s, and by the late 1840s and early '50s it had begun to have some noticeable effect. In general, however, there was not much scope in Africa for the ordinary Scot with little, if any, capital. South African farming required people with capital who could afford to employ native labour on a fairly intensive scale.

From 1854 to 1860 Sir George Grey (1812–1898), another Scot, was Governor-General of the Cape Colony, and in many ways was far ahead of his time. (Grey had a remarkable colonial career as Governor of South Australia from 1841–5, of New Zealand from 1845–53, and again from 1861–8, after South Africa. During his retirement in New Zealand he entered politics, and became Prime Minister from 1877–9.) In 1857 trouble between the Boers in the Orange Free State, newly declared a republic, and the Boers in the Transvaal reached the stage of open warfare. The Boers in the Orange Free State found themselves in such an awkward position that they approached the Cape

Sir George Grey, Governor-General of the Cape Colony, 1854–60. This extraordinary colonial administrator was also Governor of South Australia, 1841–45; and twice Governor of New Zealand, 1845–53 and again 1861–68.

Colony with a view to confederation. This met with Sir George Grey's complete approval, and he prepared a scheme for the British government accordingly, but it was rejected. By his vigorous support of missionaries such as Robert Moffat and David Livingstone, however, he managed to keep open the roads through Bechuanaland into the interior, without resorting to arms.

A contemporary Scottish explorer further north in Africa was James Grant, who came from Nairn. In association with John Speke he explored the sources of the Nile in the years 1860–63, and together they crossed equatorial Africa, being the first Europeans to accomplish this feat. In 1864 Grant published a book entitled simply and succinctly *A Walk Across Africa*.

The Niger, which had originally been explored by the Scots Mungo Park and Hugh Clapperton, who both lost their lives in their attempts, was tackled in 1861 by Macgregor Laird, son of the Clyde shipbuilder. Accompanied by Richard Lander, he led a small party with two steamships. Lander was killed and Laird's health impaired, but he formed the African Steamship Company to develop the coastal trade of West Africa, as well as sending a steamship under the command of a Scot, William Blaikie, to explore the Niger further. By building up trading depots, this venture proved successful. Laird died in 1861 and Blaikie in 1864, but in the 1880s the United Africa Company was formed and maintained the British interest in the lower Niger. It was owing to their work that the colony of Nigeria was formed.

It was not until the discovery of diamonds in Kimberley in 1866, and of gold in the Transvaal in the 1880s, that emigration to South Africa finally began to compare with that to Australia, New Zealand, or Canada. Meanwhile, through vacillation and pusillanimous government, the situation between Boers and British had grown steadily worse. In 1877 the Transvaal had been reannexed; in 1879 came the Zulu War, with some setbacks before the Zulus were defeated. Finally, in 1880, came the first Boer War, when the Boers in the Transvaal revolted and at Majuba Hill routed a small British force, to the consternation of the public at home. Despite much jingoism, Gladstone came to terms with the Boer leader, Paul Kruger, and granted the Boers independence again.

With the discovery of gold on the Witwatersrand in 1886, British, Americans, and Europeans flocked to the goldfields. Looked on with disfavour by the Boer government, they were heavily taxed and denied voting rights, for the wider outlook which might have tried to win over the 'Uitlanders' was entirely lacking from the narrow Boer mentality. They were extremely clannish, and only the Scots ministers and a few other Scots seem to have been able to integrate with them.

In 1889 Cecil Rhodes formed the British South African

Company. Dr L. S. Jameson, Rhodes's great friend, fought a campaign against the Matabele in 1893 and occupied Bulawayo. A year later the country was named Rhodesia. At this stage Rhodes was doing his best to prove to the Cape Colonists that what was being done in the north would be to their eventual advantage. Unfortunately he failed to prevent the fast accelerating distrust between British and Boer. There followed the farce of the Jameson Raid, when Dr Jameson, with 700 followers, rode to Johannesburg expecting the Uitlanders to rise with him and overthrow the Boer government. The impetuous Scottish doctor was to find no support, and he and his party were forced to surrender ignominiously and taken prisoner. This in turn brought about Rhodes's resignation.

Relations between the Orange Free State and Britain remained friendly, despite the strains between Britain and the Transvaal. President Brand of the Orange Free State, supported by John G. Fraser (later Sir John), son of a Presbyterian minister who had joined the Dutch Reformed Church, did his best to keep the nationalists under control. At his death, John G. Fraser was the unsuccessful candidate for the OFS presidency in 1896, and thereafter the Orange Free State and the Transvaal acted more or less in unison.

By 1899 the Boers, in the mood for a trial of strength, handed an ultimatum to the British who had been protesting about the treatment of the Uitlanders. The result was the second Boer War, which was to last for two and a half years and reflect little credit on either side – although the spectacle of the small Boer Republic standing up to the great British Empire and giving their armed might a salutary lesson in guerrilla warfare, caused the world to laugh openly.

It was a Scot, Sir Henry Campbell-Bannerman, as Prime Minister of Britain, who decided that the Boers should have self-government in 1906. It was, however, Dr Jameson, by this time premier of the Cape Colony, who reopened the question of federation. In 1908 an inter-colonial conference was held and a draft constitution was prepared in 1909, resulting in the formation of the Union of South Africa in 1910. The first Governor-General was another Scot, Lord Gladstone of Lanark.

Mention must be made at this point of that remarkable woman, Mary Slessor, a mill-girl turned missionary born in Dundee, who educated herself so that she could go out to Old Calabar (Nigeria), under the auspices of the United Presbyterian Church. The district of Okoyong where she settled was probably its most westerly and dangerous outpost. When the British government took over Nigeria, Mary Slessor realized that the people were not ready for new laws, and the authorities (in the shape of the Governor-General, Sir Claude Macdonald, a fellow Scot) set her in charge of the district, empowering her to preside over a native court, knowing that she had the confidence of the chiefs. She habitually spoke in broad Scots and was quite capable of boxing the ears of a native chief if she felt he deserved it, but she had the complete devotion of thousands of natives, and her career only ended with her death in 1915.

During the 1914–18 Great War the South Africans joined the British Empire without hesitation, and the Boers, erstwhile enemies, were soon fighting side-by-side with the British forces in Mesopotamia and in France. Amongst the forces raised at this time there was, almost inevitably, the South African Scottish. Although the English-speaking South Africans never numbered very much more than a million people, there were many Scots prominent amongst them.

With the outbreak of the Second World War in 1939, the Dominion of South Africa and Rhodesia, along with the other African Colonies, came once again to the support of Britain and emigrant Scots returned to fight alongside their kin. When the war ended in 1945 there was a considerable upsurge of interest in emigrating to South Africa and Rhodesia: 27,726 British emigrated to South Africa in 1948, more than went to the United States of America. The numbers emigrating to Rhodesia in the same year were 4,500, not far short of those going to New Zealand. In the following year, however, the figures for South Africa had dropped significantly, to 11,367, but those for Rhodesia remained reasonably constant at 3,916.

Following the breakaway of South Africa from the Commonwealth and the formation of the Republic in 1961, the African split with Britain grew more apparent. The independence of Nigeria, Kenya, and Uganda followed each other closely. Rhodesia's unilateral declaration of independence in 1965 should really have surprised no one, for there were enough Scots still there, and elsewhere in Africa, as advisers, administrators, or settlers, to encourage a spirit of independence. In the new state of Zimbabwe and in Africa as a whole the Scots have proved that they can still adapt to changing conditions. A natural sympathy with tribal pride and with a national desire for freedom is understandable in the emigrant Scot.

Bibliography

BERG, G., *Scots in Sweden*, Stockholm, 1962.

BLACK, GEORGE F., *Scotland's Mark on America*, New York, 1921.

BOSWELL, JAMES, *Journey to the Western Islands of Scotland*, OUP, 1924.

BRADLEY, A. G., *The United Empire Loyalists*, London, 1932.

BURT, EDWARD, CAPTAIN, *Letters*, ed. R. Jamieson, London, 1754.

BURTON, J. H., *The Scot Abroad*, Edinburgh, 1881.

CAMPBELL, C. T., *British South Africa*, London, 1897.

CAMPBELL, R. H., *Scotland since 1707*, Oxford, 1965.

CARROTHERS, W. A., *Emigration from the British Isles*, London, 1929.

DONALDSON, GORDON, *The Scot Overseas*, London, 1966.

DUNN, C. W., *Highland Settler*, Toronto, 1953.

FISCHER, T. A., *The Scots in Germany*, Edinburgh, 1902.

GIBBON, J. M., *The Scots in Canada*, London, 1911.

GRAHAM, IAN C., *Colonists from Scotland*, Ithaca, 1956.

GRAY, JOHN M., *Lord Selkirk of Red River*, London, 1963.

GRAY, M., *The Highland Economy*, Edinburgh, 1957.

HARRISON, J., *The Scot in Ulster*, Edinburgh, 1888.

HATTERSLEY, ALAN F., *The British Settlement of Natal*, Cambridge, 1950.

HILL, DOUGLAS, *Great Emigrations. The Scots to Canada*, London, 1972.

HILL, G., *The Plantation of Ulster*, Belfast, 1877.

INSH, G. P., *Scottish Colonial Schemes*, Glasgow, 1922.

JOHNSON, S. C., *Emigration from the U.K. to N. America*, London, 1913.

KIDDLE, M., *Men of Yesterday*, Melbourne, 1961.

MACDONNELL, J. A., *The Early History and Settlement of Glengarry*, Montreal, 1893.

MCLINTOCK, A. H., *The History of Otago*, Dunedin, 1949.

MICHEL, F., *Les Ecossais en France*, 2 Vols, London, 1862.

MORRISON, DAVID BAILEY, *The History of the St Andrew Society of The State of New York*, New York, 1956.

PERCEVAL-MAXWELL, M., *The Scottish Migration to Ulster*, London, 1973.

RATTRAY, W. J., *The Scot in British N. America*, 4 Vols, Edinburgh, 1880.

REED, A. H., *The Story of Early Dunedin*, Wellington, 1956.

RICH, E. E., *The History of the Hudson Bay Company*, 2 Vols, London, 1958.

SERLE, P., *A Dictionary of Australian Biography*, 2 Vols, Sydney, 1949.

STANFORD-REID, W. (ed.), *The Scottish Tradition in Canada*, Ontario, 1976.

STEUART, A. F., *The Scots in Poland*, Edinburgh, 1913.

WALSHAW, R. S., *Migration to and from the British Isles*, London, 1941.

WARBURTON, A., *A History of Prince Edward Island*, St John, New Brunswick, 1923.

Index